CW01347863

Chaucer's
The Legend of
CLEOPATRA

Geoffrey Chaucer

© *Marius Press. From an old print (Author's archive)*

Chaucer's
The Legend of
CLEOPATRA

Neil Johnson

Foreword by
Willow Sainsbury

Marius Press

Copyright © Marius Press, 2016
11 Kirklands Road, Over Kellet, Carnforth,
Lancashire LA6 1DP, UK

First edition 2015
Second edition 2016

Neil Johnson has asserted his moral right to be identified as the author of this work in accordance with the Copyright, Designs and Patents Act 1988.

A CIP catalogue record is available from the British Library.

ISBN 978-1-871622-92-8

All rights reserved. No part of this publication may be reproduced, stored in a retrieval system, or transmitted in any form or by any means, electronic, mechanical, photocopying, recording or otherwise, without prior written permission of the Publisher. No part of the text shall be sold or disposed of otherwise than as a complete book, and any unauthorised sale of such part book shall be deemed to be a breach of the Publisher's copyright. This book is sold subject to the condition that it shall not, by way of trade or otherwise, be lent, resold, hired out, or otherwise circulated, without the Publisher's prior written consent, in any form of binding or cover other than that in which it is published, and without a similar condition, including this condition, being imposed upon the subsequent purchaser.

Cover illustration

Cleopatra Adorning the Tomb of Mark Antony (1769–1770)
by Angelica Kauffman

©The Burghley House Collection, Stamford, Lincolnshire

Designed by The Drawing Room Design, Over Kellet, Lancashire, UK
Typeset by Marius Press, Over Kellet, Carnforth, Lancashire, UK
Printed and bound by Berforts, Hastings, UK

Contents

Foreword	viii
Preface	xi
1. The Life and Writings of Geoffrey Chaucer	1
Chaucer's life	1
Chaucer's Middle English	11
Chaucer's contribution	12
Manuscript versions of The Legend of Cleopatra	14
2. Why Include Cleopatra in *The Legend of Good Women*?	17
The nature of The Legend of Good Women	17
The title	20
Critical reception	21
Is the The Legend of Good Women *a satirical work?*	22
Was Cleopatra a bad woman?	24
Was Cleopatra a good woman?	26
History or literature?	30
Was the Legend not primarily about Cleopatra?	32
3. Two Middle English Versions of *The Legend of Cleopatra*	33
Middle English version 1 (Skeat)	35
Middle English version 2 (Robinson)	41
Notes	46
4. Comparison and Literal Translation of the Middle English Versions	47
Line-by-line comparison	47
Notes	71
5. Glossary	89

6. Three Modern English Versions of *The Legend of Cleopatra*	101
The form of the three versions	101
Prosodic terms	101
Modern English non-rhyming version	103
Modern English rhyming version 1 (tetrameters)	109
Modern English rhyming version 2 (pentameters)	114
7. Queen Anne and *The Legend of Good Women*	119
The life of Queen Anne	119
Chronology	124
Evidence for the influence of Queen Anne	125
Conclusions	138
8. Chaucer's Account of the Battle of Actium	139
Schofield's analysis	140
Conclusions	146
9. Sources of *The Legend of Cleopatra*	149
The Roman historians	149
Lucius Annæus Florus	151
Vincent de Beauvais	151
Giovanni Boccaccio	153
10. Is *The Legend of Cleopatra* a Poetic Success?	155
11. Source Materials	167

APPENDICES

I. The Story of Cleopatra according to Lucius Annæus Florus	171
Introduction	171
The text	172
Notes	175
II. The Story of Cleopatra according to Vincent de Beauvais	177
Introduction	177
The text	178
Notes	178

III.	The Story of Cleopatra according to Giovanni Boccaccio	181
	Introduction	181
	The text	182
	Notes	188

ILLUSTRATIONS

1.	*Geoffrey Chaucer*	ii
2.	The Hoccleve portrait of Geoffrey Chaucer	x
3.	Opening lines of *The Legend of Cleopatra* (MS Fairfax 16)	xvi
4.	*Chaucer at the Court of Edward III*	7
5.	Geoffrey Chaucer's monument, Westminster Abbey	15
6.	Coin with the head of Cleopatra	28
7.	*The Dream of Fair Women*	34
8.	*La Morte di Marco Antonio (The Death of Mark Antony)*	40
9.	*Alcestis and the Winged God of Love*	46
10.	*Cleopatra on the Terraces of Philae*	54
11.	*Cleopatra's Galley at the Battle of Actium*	62
12.	*The Meeting of Antony and Cleopatra*	73
13.	*The Battle of Actium, 2 September 31 BC*	84
14.	Cartouche (name ring) of Cleopatra	100
15.	*Antony and Cleopatra Dissolving the Pearl in Wine*	108
16.	*Anne of Bohemia, Queen Consort to Richard II*	121
17.	*Richard II Wearing Coronation Robes*	128
18.	*The Deaths of Antony and Cleopatra*	138
19.	Aureus with the head of Antony	148
20.	*Cleopatra Delivers her Life to the Serpents*	157
21.	*Cleopatra and Octavian*	166
22.	*The Raising of Antony to the Upper Window of the Tomb*	170
23.	*The Egyptian Cobra*	176
24.	The *Speculum Historiale* of Vincent de Beauvais	180
25.	*Giovanni Boccaccio*	191
26.	The Chaucer family coat of arms	192

Foreword

This book takes a little-known segment of a larger poem by Geoffrey Chaucer, unpacks the context around it, and presents no fewer than five different versions of Chaucer's 126-line poem about Cleopatra. Though the project may seem esoteric, Neil Johnson has produced a quality exploration of the poem in a focused and user-friendly study which examines transcripts, historical context, the patronage of the poem, and some possible explanations for oddities in Chaucer's text. A student will find almost every imaginable detail addressed with a weighing of interesting insights; ultimately, however, the interpretation and discussion of the significance of the poem is left largely to the student.

This exploration of Chaucer through the legend of Cleopatra also allows parallels to be drawn with other depictions of the fascinating Egyptian queen in literature and art throughout the ages, thereby further illuminating Chaucer's project. The story of Antony and Cleopatra is an enduring one: themes of power, love, extravagance, images of women, and stereotypes of Eastern exoticism *versus* Western military precision, continue to resonate.

Chaucer's representation of Cleopatra is also surprisingly modern, focusing on the equality and intensity of love in the relationship between Antony and Cleopatra. Johnson gives an interesting explanation for how this fits within Chaucer's larger project – *The Legend of Good Women*. Chaucer also injects a moral humour into this portrayal. This is not about power and manipulation, as it is seen in Shakespeare's treatment, or about the serious threat that the Romans presented, so much as about the intensity of love.

This book appears at a time of ongoing educational debate about the role of Classics, or Classical Studies, in the education curriculum. Less than 50 years ago, every student engaged in a European-style education would have had some familiarity with a certain canon of literature which included Chaucer. Many commentators have, however, remarked that in a post-colonial world, with an ever-changing technological landscape, such themes are widely outdated and even oppressive, and whilst the sentiment may be correct, the downside is that I myself have spent over 15 years in tertiary education without ever encountering Chaucer – although I recognised that, being a teacher of English, Classical Studies and History, I ought to know enough to understand why Chaucer has been studied for close to one-and-a-half millennia. By avoiding the canon of traditional Classics in schools, we may well be creating another level of an education inferiority complex. If so, the answer would seem to be to revolutionize the way in which Classics and Classical Studies are taught. Johnson's book goes some way to achieving this by examining a short segment of Chaucer's poetry within its broader context and thereby providing a way of studying Chaucer which leaves the student free to explore both Chaucer's ideas about Cleopatra and more modern interpretations of this important yet enigmatic historical figure. It is also arguable that some understanding of Middle English and its significance in the development of modern English language, is beneficial, and Johnson's book provides this, too.

Finally, and probably most importantly, the student will discover that Chaucer is not only accessible and interesting, but can even, on occasion, be funny.

Willow Sainsbury
Wellington, New Zealand, 2016.

The Hoccleve Portrait of Geoffrey Chaucer.
From *The Regiment of Princes* by Thomas Hoccleve (1410–1411)
Harley Manuscript (BL MS Harl. 4866 f 88). © British Library Board

Preface

In writing this book, I had two aims: the first was to examine one specific instance of the manner in which Queen Cleopatra of Egypt has been portrayed several centuries following the historical events in which she was involved; the second was to play my part, if at all possible, in reawakening interest in the work of Geoffrey Chaucer amongst a generation of students to whom his writings have for too long been quite literally a closed book.

Chaucer's short poem *The Legend of Cleopatra* is ideally suited to both purposes, not only because it represents the first major literary treatment of Cleopatra in the English language, but also because the process of setting the work into its proper literary context involves looking at the historical background to both the poem and the much longer work, *The Legend of Good Women*, of which it forms a small but important part.

The material chosen for inclusion has been selected from the large body of literature available on Chaucer and his work, and has been subjected to a level of analysis limited by the need to present it to readers new to Chaucer and unfamiliar with the language in which he wrote. I therefore make no claim to having produced a definitive or particularly original analysis of *The Legend of Cleopatra*, much less to having developed any novel interpretation of Chaucer's motivations for writing it. For those wishing to penetrate more deeply into such matters, there exist many detailed and scholarly considerations of this and other poems by Chaucer, both in the academic journals and in various excellent texts, some of which are noted at the end of this book in the list of the various sources upon which the present account has been based.

Willow Sainsbury has alluded in her *Foreword* to the serious reverse which the study of Chaucer has suffered in schools and in colleges in the past five decades or so, and accordingly in this book I have given a brief introduction to the English language in the form that it took between the twelfth and fifteenth centuries (Middle English, as it is now called) for those who may not already be familiar with it.

It is my hope that this book may go some way to fulfilling the laudable aim of the *New Chaucer Society* of encouraging others to extend their acquaintance with the writings of this most remarkable man who made a crucial contribution to the development of our present-day English language. Information about the *New Chaucer Society* can be found on the website: *http://newchaucersociety.org.*

Structure of the book

The book commences with a brief overview of Chaucer's life and his contribution to English poetry, followed by a note regarding the manuscripts of *The Legend of Good Women* which still exist. Next, an account of *The Legend of Good Women* focuses upon the nature of the poem and upon uncertainties which exist regarding the title; the question is also posed as to why Chaucer should have chosen to include Cleopatra – on the face of it, at least, a most unlikely candidate for the title of "good woman" – in this work.

Two slightly different texts of *The Legend of Cleopatra* in Middle English are presented, the first being that put forward in 1884 and 1889 by W. W. Skeat, and the second the version published in 1933 in *The Complete Works of Geoffrey Chaucer* edited by F. N. Robinson, and later in the 2008 edition of *The Riverside Chaucer* under the general editorship of L. D. Benson.

I compare these two Middle English versions, line by line, and give my word-by-word translations of the Middle English into Modern English. My rephrasings of the Modern English into rather more meaningful phrases or sentences then follow, with superscripts referring to explanatory notes (though these, being brief, in no way represent a detailed textual analysis). A glossary is provided of those Middle English words which have spellings differing from their modern English equivalents, or meanings which may not be immediately obvious.

I then use the Modern English expressions noted in the comparison of the Skeat and Robinsion texts (with a number of quite small clarifying adjustments) in a version of *The Legend of Cleopatra* in non-rhyming, non-metric couplets. This is followed by two new Modern English rhyming versions, the first being constructed as a series of couplets in the form of iambic tetrameters, and the second with couplets of iambic pentameters. This latter verse form – the "heroic couplet" as it is sometimes called – is particularly significant, having been introduced into English poetry by Chaucer and used by him in both *The Legend of Good Women* and *The Canterbury Tales*. Whilst neither of the two Modern English rhyming versions is presented as, or intended to be, a *formal* translation of the Middle English, together they may – or at least that is the hope – help to breathe a little freshness into *The Legend of Cleopatra*.

The intriguing suggestion is next considered that Queen Anne, the consort of Richard II, may have asked, persuaded, or even, as some writers have proposed, commanded Chaucer to write *The Legend of Good Women*. After quick overviews of Queen Anne's life and of the chronology of Chaucer's major works in the context of the reigns of Edward III and Richard II there then follows a brief examination of any evidence that may be adduced for Anne's influence. This leads on naturally to a consideration of the various sources upon which Chaucer may have relied in constructing his poem. An examination of his description of the Battle of Actium is followed by a discussion of the influences that the writings of Lucius Annæus Florus, Vincent de Beauvais, and Giovanni Boccaccio may have had on Chaucer's depiction of Cleopatra; excerpts from the writings of each of these follow in three appendices to the main text.

After a critical eye has thus been cast upon *The Legend of Cleopatra*, and the question asked as to whether or not, from an artistic point of view, it succeeds as a poem, all the source materials used in constructing this account are listed.

Acknowledgements

I would like to express my thanks first and foremost to Willow Sainsbury, whose enthusiasm for the study of Cleopatra was the primary stimulus for my writing this book. I am grateful to her for her gracious *Foreword*, and especially for her many helpful comments on my early drafts, all of which comments led, without exception, to significant improvements in the final product.

Of course, I unhesitatingly acknowledge my profound debt to all those eminent Chaucer scholars, past and present, who have written extensively and so lucidly about Chaucer's work, ideas and motivations, and upon whose writings I have drawn freely.

I am particularly indebted to my very good friend John McCormick who so unhesitatingly offered his invaluable assistance in translating a part of the *Speculum Historiale* from its original Mediæval Latin, and also for sharing with me his thoughts about both Cleopatra and Chaucer.

I have had the great pleasure of interacting with a large number of exceptionally helpful people, who either provided images presented in this book and the permission to use them, or assisted me in locating them. In particular, my thanks are due to Jackie Brown (British Library), Ryan Clee (National Galleries of Scotland), Christine Reynolds (Westminster Abbey), Graham Nisbet (Hunterian Museum), Louisa Dare (Courtauld Institute of Art), Siân Philips (Bridgeman Art Library), Sarah Miller (Heritage Auctions), Jackson Pearce White (Victoria and Albert Museum), Emma Lefley (National Maritime Museum), Jon Culverhouse (Burghley House, Lincolnshire), Alia Nour-Elsayed (Dahesh Museum of Art), Domniki Papadimitriou (Birmingham Museums Trust), Tricia Buckingham (Bodleian Library) and Jen Burford (Bodleian Library).

It is with both gratitude and admiration that I acknowledge the contribution of Graham Agnew, who once again brought his formidable graphic design expertise to bear on the project.

My wife Susan, who was meticulous in reading drafts at all stages, and made many valuable suggestions (including those for trimming my convoluted sentences), bore with exceptional fortitude my absorption over several months in what I readily acknowledge to have been a somewhat arcane pursuit.

Finally, I must record my deepest appreciation of those dedicated teachers of English, and most particularly the late Mr Geoffrey Hancock, who, in the course of my education at Sandbach School in Cheshire, introduced me to Chaucer and his Middle English writings. As all those teachers were well aware (though I, at that time, was not), there are some things which, though costing nothing, are beyond price.

Neil Johnson
Over Kellet, 2016

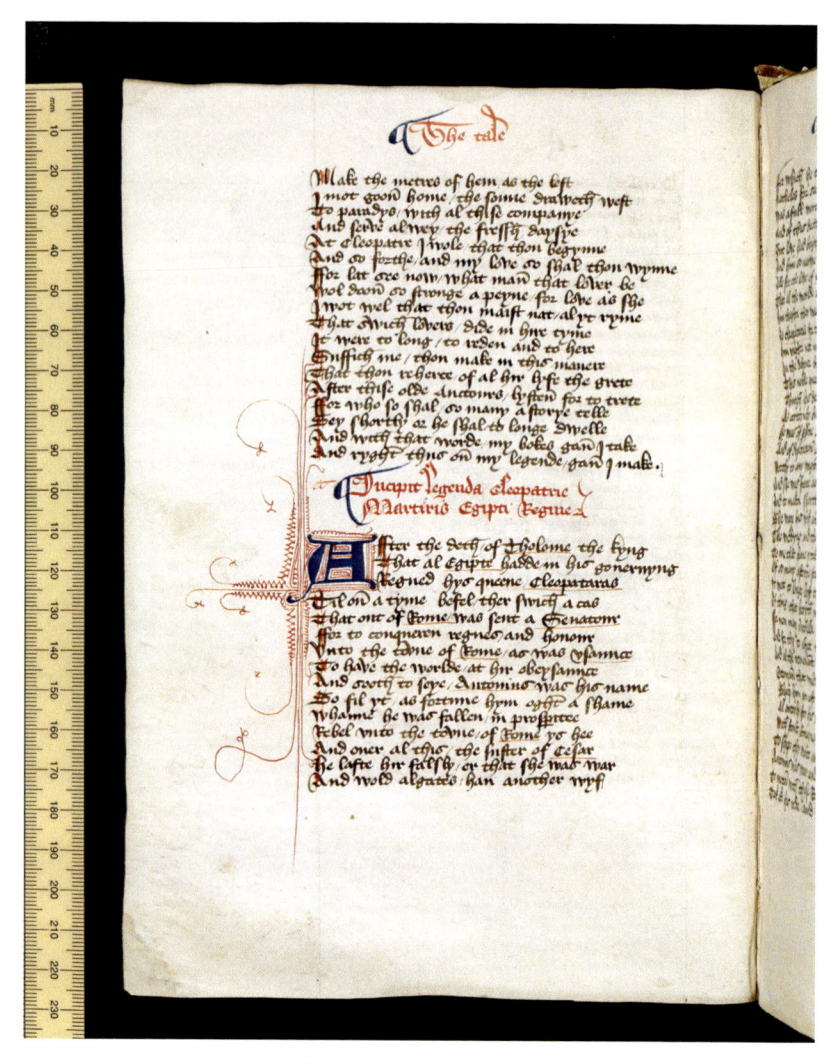

Opening lines of The Legend of Cleopatra
MS Fairfax 16 (90v) (ca 1450)
© Bodleian Library, Oxford

1

The Life and Writings of Geoffrey Chaucer

Chaucer's life

Geoffrey Chaucer was born in London at some time between 1340 and 1344: the precise date is uncertain, though the former is regarded as the more likely. It has been suggested – again the record is not always reliable on such matters – that his grandfather Robert le Chaucer worked with the Customs in relation to wine imported from Aquitaine. This certainly seems plausible, Geoffrey's father John Chaucer being a vintner – a seller and possibly importer of wine (and not, as has been claimed by some writers, an inn-keeper) and also having some function associated with the collection of customs duties on the exportation of cloth from a number of ports.

The circumstances surrounding Geoffrey's early life are obscure, apart from the fact that he probably spent the greater part of his childhood in the family home at 177 Upper Thames Street in London, where he was born.

Of his early education even less is known, though a great deal has been speculated. It is likely that he either attended one of the schools in the parish of St Martin in the Vintny Ward, where his home was situated, or that he received his education at home, possibly from a hired tutor. Though some teaching would have been in English, much would have been in French which, some three-hundred years after the Norman conquest in 1066, had become the language both of government and of the educated and aristocratic classes. In addition, pupils would have had to acquire a knowledge of Latin, both written and spoken, as this would have been employed not only in eclesiastical circles, but also in the conduct of legal matters, trade and commerce throughout Europe.

Geoffrey's family certainly possessed ample financial resources, his father having inherited properties from relatives and also being (as most vintners were) wealthy in his own right and socially well-placed. As Geoffrey's mother Agnes had also inherited some properties, she too was financially comfortable. Despite his parents' evident ability to support their son's attendance at a university, there is no record of Geoffrey's having taken his education quite that far; and there are, indeed, some who suggest that what seems to have been his relatively superficial acquaintance with many of the stories and those historical or mythological figures about whom he composed much of his poetry argues against his ever having attained a particularly high level of learning. He appears to have been oblivious to historical inaccuracies which his work all too often contained, and was also given to occasional misreadings of Latin works on which his own writings were based. Brewer (1978) says:

> Chaucer's knowledge of Latin must not be exaggerated. Many of his references to Latin literature could have come from a few anthology volumes. He never read Latin fluently, or very accurately ....
> *Brewer (1978)*

One might, however, take issue with this conclusion. After all, as will be mentioned later, Chaucer's employment in the country's Customs would necessarily have involved familiarity with international commerce and all the various limitations on its legality, and his eventual engagement as the King's Clerk of Works would have required him to be conversant with mathematics and the law – all of which would have been possible only if he had possessed a reasonably good command of Latin. Certainly, many of his writings reveal an acquaintance with legal conduct, for which a fairly high degree of competency in Latin would have been essential. Most compelling, however, is the fact that he incorporated into some of his works (most notably in the *Man of Law's Tale* and its *Prologue*) translations of parts of *De Miseria Condicionis Humane* by Pope Innocent III, which had originally been written in Latin; and then in 1390, ten years before his death, it appears – according to a passage in the *Prologue* to *The Legend of Good Women* – that he also went on to translate the whole of *De Miseria Condicionis Humane*, to which he gave the title *Of the Wretched Engendrynge of Mankynde* (this being one of Chaucer's lost works).

Even the historical inaccuracy of some of Chaucer's writings does not necessarily argue against his having had some degree of higher education. At that time, the doings and personal characteristics of historical figures were very often treated as though those figures were more mythological than actual, resulting in their being given romantic gloss and dramatic colouring; strict adherence to historical accuracy was not accorded the importance that is now attached to it (see also pp. 30–32).

Chaucer's father was eventually engaged by the royal household, becoming deputy to the butler of King Edward III. Being a butler did not imply having the kind of duties which we would now associate with the title, but involved being the primary purchasing agent of the household's wine – a most suitable task for a vintner. In due course, Chaucer, like his father, was taken into the royal household, and entered into the service of Elizabeth de Burgh, Countess of Ulster, as a pageboy, probably around 1354 when he would have been about fourteen years of age. Her first husband, the Earl of Ulster, having been murdered, Elizabeth had returned to England from Ireland and, in due course, had married Prince Lionel of Antwerp, the third son of Edward III and Queen Philippa, and older brother of John of Gaunt.

In the cultured atmosphere in which he now found himself, Chaucer would have been required to familiarise himself with all the manners and conventions of courtly conduct, and would also have had ample opportunity to improve his use of everyday Latin and French.

In due course, he became a yeoman in the service of Prince Lionel, and it was in this capacity that in 1359 he found himself fighting in France, where he was taken prisoner, eventually being ransomed on 1 March, 1360 (Edward III is said to have made a contribution of £16 to the ransom). That same year, Chaucer returned to France carrying, on behalf of Prince Lionel, letters which may have been related to the Treaty of Breigny.

It was in the 1360s that Chaucer translated, from French into English, *Roman de la Rose*, a long French love poem, the first 4,000 lines of which had been written by Guillaume de Lorris around 1235, with the remaining 18,000 lines being contributed by Jean de Meun (see pp. 145 & 146) some 40 years later. That he was sufficiently confident to produce this translation (as *Romaunt of the Rose*) is indicative of Chaucer's close acquaintance with French. It also established his reputation as a poet.

When John Chaucer died in 1366, he left a widow and his son Geoffrey, who, as far as it is possible to tell from the historical records, appears to have been the only child of the marriage. This may also have been the year in which Chaucer married. Very little is known of Chaucer's wife, except that her name, like that of the queen, was Philippa; she was probably Philippa de Roet, one of the ladies-in-waiting to Queen Philippa and also the sister of Katherine Swynford who was the third wife of John of Gaunt (Duke of Lancaster and possibly the richest man in the land). The marriage between Chaucer and Philippa produced a son whom they named Lewis; although it seems that there may have been other children (some accounts list as many as four), nothing is known about them. It was possibly through his marriage to Philippa that Chaucer became drawn into the service of Edward III, to whom he acted first as a valet (*vallectus*) in 1367, and then, one year later, as an Esquire.

A number of trips that Chaucer is known to have made between 1369 and 1378 to both France and Italy (specifically to Genoa, Pisa and Florence), and perhaps also to a number of other European destinations, have been taken as evidence that he was employed in some form of diplomatic, and possibly intelligence-gathering, activity, probably at the behest of his wife's brother-in-law John of Gaunt who, as Rudd (2001) has pointed out, had become an important figure in Chaucer's life. In 1368, John of Gaunt's first wife Blanche had died, aged

Chaucer at the Court of Edward III
Ford Madox Brown, 1854
© *Birmingham Museums Trust*

Chaucer's poems were written to be read to an audience, the great majority of the population being unable to read, and the few manuscript versions of the poems very expensive. This watercolour shows Chaucer reading, presumably from one of his early works, to an enthralled audience. With the exception of Edward III on his throne, it is not possible to identify with certainty the others shown here. The lady on Edward's left hand wearing a crown may be Queen Philippa. On Edward's right, the helmeted figure could be either Edward of Woodstock (the Black Prince) or John of Gaunt, whilst the man in blue in the foreground could be Prince Lionel.

only 28, prompting Chaucer to write *The Book of the Duchess* (sometimes called *The Deth of Blaunche*); it may have been in recognition of this that, around 1374, John of Gaunt granted him an annuity of £10. *The Book of the Duchess*, like *Romaunt of the Rose* before it, served to mark out Chaucer as a major literary figure of his time.

With regard to possible covert aspects of Chaucer's foreign trips, it is known that in 1376 he accompanied Sir John Burley upon a mission of undisclosed purpose, and that later he went with others to Flanders and France to negotiate peace. Chaucer's visits to Italy, also on the king's secret affairs, suggest that he may have had some proficiency in speaking Italian; certainly, it is known that, whilst in Florence, he purchased a number of Italian poetry books – though the possibility that he also met Boccaccio or Petrarch, both living in Italy at that time, is regarded by some (e.g., Rudd, 2001) as fairly remote. Although Boccaccio had been employed around 1340–1341 by the authorities in Florence to conduct missions of a diplomatic character and might therefore have been moving in the same circles as those with whom Chaucer made contact, Rudd makes the point that Chaucer's writings at this time seem to have owed more to the influence of Dante, and that it was only after he had made a visit to Milan in 1378 that Chaucer's work began to reflect some aspects of the style either of Petrarch or of

Boccaccio, both of whom were no longer alive – Petrarch, having died in 1374 and Boccaccio in 1375 (see also pp. 153 & 154, and Appendix III).

In 1374, Chaucer became Comptroller of Customs and Subsidies (Wools, Skins and Hides) in the Port of London, and later, in 1382, Comptroller of the Petty Customs on Wines and Merchandise. He was appointed Justice of the Peace for Kent in 1385 and, the following year, a Knight of the Shire for that county, thus automatically becoming a Member of Parliament; both appointments indicate that by this time he was a man of some substance, and most probably a landowner.

By late 1386 or early 1387, however, Chaucer had left his positions with the Port of London, and was no longer a Justice of the Peace or Member of Parliament. This may have been because his wife Philippa died around that time, or perhaps because he found it too onerous to act in public capacities carrying high degrees of responsibility. In any case, by this time his status as a major poet had been confirmed by his *Parlement of Foules*, *The House of Fame*, *Anelida and Arcite* and *Troilus and Criseyde*.

Chaucer's decision to leave public life may also have been related to changes in the royal power structure in England. Edward III had died ten years earlier, and his grandson Richard had ascended the throne. The young Richard II and his equally young wife Anne were now well established at the head of the royal household. It seems clear that Chaucer must have been well known to the royal couple. Richard, for example, would surely have been consulted when, in 1389, Chaucer was offered the position of Clerk of the King's Works at Westminster, the Tower of London, and eight of the royal residences. Among the residences which were overseen by Chaucer were the manor houses at Eltham and Sheen – which is a matter of some significance, as will be seen later (Ch. 7, p. 129). Around the time that he assumed the position of Clerk of the King's Works, he began writing *The Legend of Good Women*, which was followed by – and possibly overlapped with – his best-known work, *The Canterbury Tales*.

In 1391, the year in which he completed his *Treatise on the Astrolabe*, Chaucer relinquished his post as Clerk of the King's Works for reasons which have been a matter of considerable speculation, but which in all probability had much to do with his having been violently robbed on three occasions in the past twelve months.

Whilst in employment he had accrued debts on behalf of the Crown and these he had to pay back out of his own funds in a series of instalments over the ensuing years. Although his financial situation may therefore seem to have been somewhat precarious, he was in fact receiving an annuity of £20 from Richard II as well as financial or material support from a number of other sources, and this was supplemented by an income from his new position as Deputy Forester for North Pemberton, a post which he had taken up at some time after 1391.

Beyond this, little is known of his final years, or of any effect upon him of the overthrow in 1399 of Richard II by Henry Bolingbroke, the son of John of Gaunt.

Geoffrey Chaucer died on 25 October 1400.

Chaucer's Middle English

The evolution of the English language is usually regarded as having three stages. *Old English*, which was spoken until about 1100, was distinctly Germanic in structure and pronunciation. After the Norman conquest in 1066, Norman French had become the language of government and commerce and of the educated classes, eventually permeating throughout everyday speech; not only was much of the inflected Germanic grammar thereby lost, being replaced by a much simpler structure, but a rich vocabulary of new, Latin-based words was introduced.

The much-changed language of this period became what we now call *Middle English*. This, too, was gradually transformed as its usage extended beyond the governing classes, developing eventually into *Modern English*.

Although the Modern English period is usually defined as commencing around 1500, the next five centuries saw substantial changes, as the language as it was spoken by

Shakespeare, Milton, Byron and Austen evolved – aided in no small part by the development of printing – into our familiar tongue.

Until Chaucer began to produce his major works, prose writing in England had been mainly in Latin, with some also in the French of the Norman conquerors; any prose in English was primarily for ecclesiastical purposes. Spoken Middle English, a rich amalgam of Anglo-Saxon and Norman French, which spread so rapidly across the country in the thirteenth and fourteenth centuries, was far from being a unified language, being divided into a variety of very different regional dialects. Moreover, the rules of English spelling, for such small quantities of prose as were produced, were not universally recognized: indeed, a codified system of "correct" spelling would not emerge until several centuries later.

Naturally, Chaucer, who had been born and brought up in London, wrote and spelt (though not always consistently) in the everyday dialect of the capital city, thus making his works immediately intelligible – to those who could read – to the largest concentration of population in England.

Chaucer's contribution

It would be difficult to overemphasize the importance of Chaucer in the history of English literature, particularly

English poetry. For his establishment of London-English as the basic medium for literary expression, Chaucer has rightly become regarded as the father of modern written and spoken English. Not only that, but he introduced into English poetry at least twelve different meters (reading rhythms) – about which we shall have rather more to say later (see pp. 101–102). Though these, like some other aspects of his verse structure, were derived mainly from French, and possibly also Italian, poetical works, they were employed by Chaucer to demonstrate that English could be used – and to great effect – as a poetic language in its own right.

Poetry in Old English was quite different from that seen in the later periods of the language's development. Being heavily inflected (the grammatical function of a word being signified by changes in, or additions to, the word's ending), Old English did not readily lend itself to the construction of rhyme. Poetry was therefore limited to the heavy use of alliteration – the linking of words by their initial letters or sounds ("frolicking freely in the fertile fields," for example, or "something sumptuous in summer's slumbers").

When the burden of inflection was lost, and rhyming thus became as easily achievable in Middle English as it already was in French and Italian, Chaucer and others, whilst never entirely abandoning alliteration as a device, embraced rhyming enthusiastically. Chaucer, in addition to developing the new Middle English poetic form by his introduction of different meters, also created the "heroic couplet," which consisted of a pair of rhyming lines with a defined rhythm, the *iambic pentameter* (p. 102); for this reason, Chaucer may fairly be described not only as the father of Modern English, as noted earlier, but as the father of English poetry, too.

When he died in 1400 he was interred in Westminster Abbey in an area which was reserved for royal servants. His great contribution to English literature was acknowledged in 1566, when his remains were transferred to an ornate tomb in that part of the Abbey which has since become known as Poets' Corner. Chaucer was the first poet to be honoured in this way.

Manuscript versions of The Legend of Cleopatra

Chaucer's writings preceded the widespread use of the printing press by at least half a century (William Caxton, the first English printer, was born some twenty or more years after Chaucer's death), and thus the earliest manuscripts of his which still exist are all hand-produced copies. Inevitably, as copy after copy was made, changes occurred – particularly in spelling, for which, as we have already noted, such principles as existed were relatively few and loosely framed.

Geoffrey Chaucer's Monument,
Poets' Corner, Westminster Abbey, London.
© Marius Press. From an old print (Author's archive)

The scribes employed to make these serial copies may ocasionally have become bored or distracted, missing out, or perhaps repeating, words or whole lines; they may also have been inclined to adjust Chaucer's London-English spelling so that it was nearer to their own regional dialect, and thereby possibly destroying some subtle poetic effect which Chaucer had intended. Inevitably, too, many of the manuscripts would have suffered some degree of damage over time, and pages would have been lost from them.

Chaucer's *The Legend of Cleopatra*

Today, there exist twelve or thirteen manuscripts, of variable quality, completeness and authenticity, of *The Legend of Good Women*, though *The Legend of Cleopatra* does not appear in all. Most scholarly attention has been directed towards six or eight of them. The four referred to, respectively, as the *Fairfax 16* (see the illustration on p. xvi), the *Cambridge Gg 4.27*, the *Ellesmere*, and the *Hengwrt*, are probably the most widely used and relied upon. The relationships between the various manuscripts have been analysed in detail by Amy (1918).

The Middle English versions of *The Legend of Cleopatra* which are presented later in this book are based upon the first two of the manuscripts noted above, i.e., *Fairfax 16*, carrying a date of 1450 and currently held by the Bodleian Library, Oxford, and the *Cambridge Gg 4.27*, which appears to have been produced at some time between 1430 and 1440 and is in the University Library, Cambridge: which of these two may be the nearer to Chaucer's original is hard to say. We have always to bear in mind the point made by Burnley (1983), that:

> ... editors have had to admit that the full restoration of Chaucer's original is impossible: the best that can be done is to produce a version one stage closer to the original than the best existing copy. However, the selection of this "best manuscript" is not an infallible process and may be fraught with controversy.
>
> *Burnley (1983).*

2

Why Include Cleopatra in *The Legend of Good Women*?

The nature of The Legend of Good Women

The Legend of Good Women is composed of a *Prologue*, the content of which differs markedly from one manuscript to another (see p. 129), followed by a series of 13 poems, or *legends*, of "good women." *The Legend of Cleopatra* is the first, and also, with only 126 lines (127 if one counts the final "Amen" – see p. 88), the shortest of these. Cleopatra is, moreover, the only one of the nine women presented who was a real character in history, rather than someone who featured solely in myth – though Chaucer's treatment of her story, or rather the small aspect of her story which he selected, is actually more mythological than factual in style (see pp. 30–31).

Numerous commentators have found it curious, to say the least, that Chaucer should have included Cleopatra under the general rubric of "good women":

> Chaucer began his series of legends with an odd choice and what seems on several counts an unfortunate choice.
>
> *Frank (1972)*

Chaucer's *The Legend of Cleopatra*

Certainly, when one thinks about the ways in which Cleopatra was portrayed by the Roman historians, some of the epithets that spring most readily to mind include *lascivious, promiscuous, wanton,* and – to go beyond the purely sexual – *scheming, single-minded, ambitious, cruel, driven, courageous, unscrupulous* – but hardly *good.*

In trying to understand why Chaucer chose Cleopatra as one of his "good women," it will be helpful to take a brief look at the nature of *The Legend of Good Women* and at the reason which is given in its *Prologue* for his having undertaken the task of writing it.

As nearly as can be determined, *The Legend of Good Women* was written around 1385 or 1386, and at the same time that Chaucer was beginning his most famous work, *The Canterbury Tales.* It is one of what are referred to collectively as Chaucer's "dream works," and in its *Prologue* Chaucer describes how, in a dream, he kneels before the god of Love, who berates him, first for having insulted women in his translation of the *Roman de la Rose,* and then for compounding the fault by enlarging yet again upon the unfaithfulness, or at least the fickleness, of women in *Troilus and Criseyde.* However, the god's beautiful consort then intercedes on Chaucer's behalf, suggesting that, since his intelligence may not have been adequate for him to write accurately on the subject of the faithfulness of women, his previous poems

Why Include Cleopatra?

had probably been composed in all innocence. She thus proposes that Chaucer be given what she feels is a light penance – that he should spend the remainder of his days in writing a legendary of Cupid's saints and, in so doing, compose a faithful record of the lives of all those women who, throughout history, had been regarded as martyrs to love. In short, he is commanded to write *The Legend of Good Women*. The god's consort says:

> The moste partye of thy tyme spende
> In making of a glorious Legende
> Of Gode Wommen, maidenes and wyves
> That weren trewe in lovinge al hir lyves;
> And telle of false men that hem bitrayen ....
> And thogh thee lyke nat a lover be,
> Spek wel of love, this penance yive I thee.
> And to the god of love I shal so preye
> That he shal charge his servants by any weye
> To forthren thee, and wel thy labour quyte.
> Go now thy wey, this penaunce is but lyte.

> *Spend the greater part of your time*
> *In writing a glorious legend*
> *Of good women, maidens and wives*
> *Who were faithful in love all their lives;*
> *And tell of the false men who betrayed them ....*
> *And though you are an unlikely lover,*
> *Speak well of love. This penance I give you.*
> *And to the god of Love I shall pray*
> *That he shall command his servants in every way*
> *To guide you, and help you to complete your work.*
> *Go now on your way; this penance is but light.*

The queen consort is then revealed as Alcestis ("I, your Alceste"), the faithful wife of Greek legend, who had died for the love of her husband (see the illustrations on pp. 34 & 46; and see also pp. 130 & 163).

At the end of the *Prologue*, the god of Love then goes on to specify how Chaucer should set about constructing *The Legend of Good Women*, instructing him that the first of the legends should be about Cleopatra:

> At Cleopatre I wol that thou beginne,
> And so forth; and my love so shal thou winne.
>
> *I wish you to begin with Cleopatra,*
> *And so proceed, so that you may win my love.*

The title

Not least of the areas of contention which surround *The Legend of Good Women* is that which relates to the title itself – a title which is, in fact, used in only two of the extant manuscripts.

In most manuscripts no title is given, whilst in one it is called *The Boke of the ix Goode Women* and in another *The Legend of Ladies*. In the *Prologue* to *The Man of Law's Tale* (one of *The Canterbury Tales*), it is referred to as *The Seintes Legend of Cupide*, whilst in the final section of *The Canterbury Tales* (referred to as the *Retraction*) it is cited as *The Book of the xxv Ladies* or, according to some other manuscripts, *the xv* or *the xiv Ladies* (see also p. 134).

Why Include Cleopatra?

Most students of Chaucer are happy to use the title *The Legend of Good Women*, primarily because, in the *Prologue* to the work, Alceste, the god of Love's consort, refers to "good women" ("Gode Wommen, maidenes and wyves"), as we have already seen in the passage quoted above (p. 19).

Critical reception

As mentioned in the *Preface* to this book, and again in Chapter 1, in terms of the development of Chaucer's own literary style *The Legend of Good Women* is particularly notable for its introduction into English poetry of the "heroic couplet," which made its triumphant reappearance in *The Canterbury Tales*. The poem nevertheless remains a literary curiosity which has long divided critical opinion, being variously judged a poetic gem or a dismal failure. Though popular and well-received when it was first written, *The Legend of Good Women* later fell into relative obscurity, arousing little academic interest. In recent years, however, things appear to have come full circle, and it has now become the subject of much scholarly discussion, the greater part of which focuses upon two versions of its *Prologue*, which were written at different times and which differ in phrasing and content in intriguing ways. Such matters, however, lie beyond the scope of the present book (though see pp. 129).

Chaucer's *The Legend of Cleopatra*

Is the Legend of Good Women *a satirical work?*

One of the most frequently offered explanations for the inclusion of Cleopatra in the *Legend of Good Women* is that Chaucer was so antipathetic to the whole idea of writing a series of poems about "good" women that he proceeded to construct the whole work as a satire, and that he did so by including some women to whom the descriptions "good," in the sense of "chaste" or "faithful" – or, indeed, other aspects of morality – hardly applied.

> One scholar has gone so far as to suggest that Chaucer composed the work from the outset with satirical purpose – writing, so to speak, with his tongue in his cheek. Some of the good women... were anything but good, being guilty of murder and other crimes. Chaucer selected and praised them [it is argued] precisely for the purpose of making his ostensible defence of women ridiculous, and so of perpetrating a huge joke upon critics and patrons.
> *Robinson (1933)*

The view that Chaucer was engaging in no more than a pretence, has also been espoused by other writers:

> Chaucer pretends to do again what his *Troilus* had supposedly failed to do: to defend a much maligned woman.
> *Quinn (1994)*

The proposal that Chaucer intended *The Legend of Good Women* to be satirical is not at all inconsistent with

Why Include Cleopatra?

the humour which is evident throughout his writings – and perhaps nowhere more so than in *The Canterbury Tales*.

> The private joke at the expense of "authority" was very much to Chaucer's taste, especially when delivered with solemnity, as when he embarked on *The Ryme of Sir Thopas* in *The Canterbury Tales*, traditional, ludicrous, and gravely given forth.
>
> *Coghill (1949)*

If humour was indeed the aim, one has to admit that Chaucer seems to have been more than a trifle heavy-handed; and it may, according to Robinson (1933), be that the suggestion is either misplaced or unnecessary:

> This attempt to find unrecognized humour in the *Legend*, and so to rescue it from the charge of dullness, even if it seemed needful, is ill-advised. For there can be no doubt that in the mind of Chaucer and his contemporaries the heroines he celebrates were good in the sense that counted for the purpose in hand – they were faithful followers of the god of Love.
>
> *Robinson (1933)*

The point is well made, and despite the scepticism expressed by some, Chaucer's choice of Cleopatra as one of the "good" women may not, at the time of writing, have been quite as paradoxical as one might at first think. He could, as Robinson suggests, merely have been following a simple brief – that of eulogizing women who had died for love – or might, at least, be represented as having done so.

Was Cleopatra a bad woman?

One can well understand the puzzlement expressed by some regarding Chaucer's inclusion of Cleopatra amongst his "Gode Wommen." After all, her extramarital affairs with both Julius Caesar and Antony (notwithstanding the assertion by Chaucer and several others that she had actually married Antony) had led to her producing children fathered by each of them. Not only that, but she had apparently also been complicit in the murders of both her half-sister Arsinoë and her brother Ptolemy XIV (who was also her husband and therefore – at least in non-Egyptian eyes – incestuously so).

Moreover, the notion that her suicide had been an act of martyrdom to love hardly appeared to withstand close scrutiny. As Chaucer would surely have been well aware, Cleopatra had been portrayed by the great majority of Roman historians as having taken her own life not from an overwhelming desire to lie beside her lover, the now dead Antony, but primarily out of self-interest – wishing, not unreasonably, to avoid the fate of being taken prisoner by Octavian, paraded as a captive in his inevitable Triumph on his return to Rome, and then, as was the custom, being ritually strangled immediately afterwards.

Why Include Cleopatra?

That Cleopatra was essentially both manipulative and insincere was a view widely held at the time that Chaucer was writing *The Legend of Good Women*. For example, the fourteenth-century Italian author and poet Giovanni Boccaccio (see Appendix III) had presented the Egyptian queen as a woman who, according to Margaret-Anne Franklin (2006), had

> ... used her seductive charms to manipulate Caesar, who then gave her the kingdom of Egypt .... With this conquest, Cleopatra launched an extended campaign of exchanging sexual favours for sovereignty, and became "the whore of the Eastern kings" .... For Boccaccio [she] was the most iniquitous of those women who, motivated by a "burning desire to rule ... [succeeded] only through wickedness."
>
> *Franklin (2006)*

Boccaccio was intensely hostile towards Cleopatra, treating her and her relationship with Antony in a highly pejorative manner, even suggesting that she may have tried to seduce Octavian after Antony's suicide – a notion which had also been entertained by earlier writers, particularly by Lucius Annæus Florus and Vincent de Beauvais (see Chapter 9, Appendices I & II, and p. 166).

Chaucer did make two relatively minor concessions to the kind of negative image that Boccaccio and others were presenting of Cleopatra. One particular line in *The Legend of Cleopatra* appears, on the face of it at least, to make a direct and very obvious reference to Cleopatra's lustfulness. As we shall see in Chapters 3 and 4 and on p. 78, Chaucer says clearly that when Cleopatra had married Antony she "had him as she desired". This was such a clear reversal of the traditional husband-and-wife dominance relationship as understood in Chaucer's time, that several of the scribes who copied manuscripts of *The Legend of Good Women* seem to have felt obliged to make some amendments, the phrasing being changed to read "had him as *he* desired" or "had him at *his* desire."

Perhaps there is another hint in Chaucer's poem of the wantonness of Cleopatra when she makes a curious interjection in her pre-suicide speech, suddenly, and as an apparent afterthought, saying "I mean you, Antony" – almost as though she wishes to make it quite clear that it is Antony, and not any one of a number of other lovers, about whom she is speaking.

With the sole exception of these lines, however, the poem says nothing further that is at all detrimental about Cleopatra's character.

Was Cleopatra a good woman?

The belief that Cleopatra was essentially bad was not shared by everyone. As Taylor (1977) has pointed out, the view of Cleopatra which was promulgated by Boccaccio, at least in the extreme form in which he expressed it, was

Why Include Cleopatra?

not the only one entertained both before and at the time of Chaucer, and that many of these other views were far from antagonistic towards the Egyptian queen.

Chaucer's own gentle treatment of Cleopatra may reflect his understanding that her portrayal at the hands of the Roman historians had been heavily influenced by the views of Octavian (the future Caesar Augustus) and of Octavian's propagandists. The question as to the sources used by Chaucer in constructing *The Legend of Cleopatra* is discussed further in Chapter 9.

Lucy Hughes-Hallett (1990) has examined in detail the story of Cleopatra according to Octavian, as well as the many falsehoods spun by him about the Egyptian queen, and which were accepted, apparently without question, not only by historians writing at that time, but subsequently by many others:

> Even before her life was over its events were being selected, falsified and otherwise tailored to fit the contours of a story – a story loosely based on actual events, but deliberately and drastically misrepresenting them .... That story was devised by Octavius [Octavian], Cleopatra's enemy, as the main vehicle for his propaganda against her and Antony .... It is a story of a great but flawed hero undone by his passion for a cunning queen .... This imaginary Cleopatra was designed to eclipse Antony, to subsume him and render him invisible.
>
> *Hughes-Hallett (1990)*

Coin with the head of Cleopatra

© *The Hunterian Museum, University of Glasgow, 2015*

This unflattering portrait of Cleopatra may have been intended to emphasize the facial characteristics of the Ptolemaic rulers.

However, as Hughes-Hallet goes on to note, a quite different picture of Cleopatra's character was sometimes painted: for example, she was referred to by the seventh-century Bishop John of Nikiu as "wise" and "courageous," and several Alexandrian scholars spoke admiringly of her scholarship and scientific knowledge. Even Cicero who, in his letters, described Cleopatra as haughty to the point of arrogance, commented on her intellectual interests.

Why Include Cleopatra?

Though accounts of Cleopatra's erudition may be just as much propaganda constructs as the stories put about by Octavian, the favourable view of her as the embodiment of female virtue, a chaste woman who sacrificed herself for love, was widely held in the Middle Ages and in the early Renaissance by a great number of dramatists and poets. Shakespeare, in *Antony and Cleopatra*, writes in such a vein when he has Cleopatra say:

> Give me my robe, put on my crown, I have
> Immortal longings in me. Now, no more
> The juice of Egypt's grape shall moist this lip –
> Yare, yare, good Iras; quick. – Methinks I hear
> Antony call: I see him rouse himself
> To praise my noble act; I hear him mock
> The luck of Caesar, which the gods give men
> To excuse their after wrath. Husband, I come:
> Now to that name my courage prove my title!
> I am fire, and air; my other elements
> I give to baser life ....
>
> *William Shakespeare (1600--1612)*

Dryden, in *All for Love; or the World Well Lost* (1678) also endorsed the view of Cleopatra as a martyr to her deep and sincere love for Antony. When asked by her handmaiden why she wishes to have "my crown and richest jewels" brought to her, Cleopatra replies:

> Dull, that thou art! why 'tis to meet my love;
> As when I saw him first, on Cydnos bank,
> All sparkling, like a goddess: so adorned,

I'll find him once again; my second spousals
Shall match my first in glory. Haste, haste, both,
And dress the bride of Antony ....

and then later, having received the asp's sting:

Already, death, I feel thee in my veins:
I go with such a will to find my lord,
That we shall quickly meet.
A heavy numbness creeps through every limb,
And now 'tis at my head: My eye-lids fall,
And my dear love is vanquish'd in a mist.
Where shall I find him, where? O turn me to him,
And lay me on his breast! – Caesar, thy worst;
Now part us, if thou canst.

John Dryden (1678)

Nevill Coghill (1949) has commented that it is:

... startling to modern taste to find Cleopatra heading the list of faithful female lovers, the proto-martyr of her sect. The Choice of Medea and Philomela, known for their horrible infanticides, is also odd; but there is evidence for thinking that in the middle ages they were among the stock examples of feminine fidelity [and there is other evidence from some] sources to show that Chaucer's choices were traditional.

Coghill (1949)

History or literature?

Of course, we shall never know what Chaucer's true reasons were, not only for taking the decision to include Cleopatra amongst his "good women," but also for putting her first in the list. Perhaps we have therefore to content

Why Include Cleopatra?

ourselves with evaluating *The Legend of Cleopatra* on the basis of literary criteria alone, i.e., purely as a poem (see Chapter 10) and not as an exercise in history.

Even if Chaucer's contemporaries and the audience for whom he was writing had felt that the infidelities and crimes of Cleopatra (or, at least, those that had, rightly or wrongly, been ascribed to her) made her inclusion in the list of "good women" incongruous, Chaucer may have felt that the emotional drama of her heroic death by the bite of an asp (or, as his poem would have it, by flinging herself naked into a pit containing many asps), and all in the name of an undying love, was so powerful and intense that it would cancel out the image which Boccaccio, amongst others, had painted of Cleopatra as a scheming and duplicitous seductress.

Perhaps such speculation is unnecessary: historical accuracy and veracity were not, after all, the primary concerns of mediæval writers and poets who aimed to represent their historical characters as essentially heroic, rather than as bearers of all the usual human frailties. The recounting of the story of Cleopatra's death *in the context of martyrdom to love* was within this tradition, whatever the objective reality of her suicide may have been. Chaucer was simply telling a *story*: he was not re-telling *history*. In such a context his portrayal of Cleopatra may not be as extraordinary as some have thought.

Was the Legend not primarily about Cleopatra?

Finally, we must consider the intriguing possibility which has been raised by Schofield (1913) regarding Chaucer's choice of Cleopatra. After presenting detailed arguments for the view that Chaucer's exceptionally vivid description of the Battle of Actium clearly embodies elements drawn directly from the kind of naval engagements which had recently taken place, or with which the maritime forces of England were being threatened in the second half of the fourteenth century, Schofield adds:

> ... one may even go so far as to suggest that the widespread interest in naval affairs in England while Chaucer was fashioning the *Legend of Good Women* may have led him to include Cleopatra among the "Saints of Cupid," though she had not previously been famed as "trewe in lovinge al hir lyve": it gave him an opportunity to describe one of the decisive battles of the world in a way that must have stirred all his associates.
>
> *Schofield (1913)*

If Schofield is correct in this – and his analysis, as will be detailed later (Chapter 8), is certainly persuasive – we may perhaps be relieved of what, at times, seems overly tortuous justification for the presence of Cleopatra in *The Legend of Good Women*.

3

Two Middle English Versions of
The Legend of Cleopatra

There now follow two Middle English texts of *The Legend of Cleopatra*. The first of these (Version 1) appeared in 1889 in Rev. Walter W. Skeat's book *Chaucer: The Legend of Good Women*. Skeat, who at that time held the post of Elrington and Bosworth Professor in Anglo-Saxon at the University of Cambridge, was a well-respected scholar of Chaucer and Middle English; he developed a version of the poem based upon the *Fairfax 16* manuscript held by the Bodleian Library in Oxford (see p. xvi), though he made a number of adjustments to spelling and punctuation in accordance with his reading of other manuscripts, where he found these to be more clearly written.

Skeat's version remained accepted as the standard text of the poem until 1933, when a newer one (Version 2) was eventually produced by F. N. Robinson, Professor of English at Harvard University. In his book *The Complete Works of Geoffrey Chaucer*, Robinson employed what is probably the earliest manuscript, the *Cambridge Gg 4.27*, to produce the version of the *Legend of Cleopatra* which is the one most widely used today.

Chaucer's *The Legend of Cleopatra*

The Dream of Fair Women
Sir Edward Coley Burne-Jones, 1865
© *The Makins Collection/Bridgeman Images*

The Legend of Good Women was the inspiration for Tennyson's *A Dream of Fair Women*, on which Burne-Jones' painting was based. Alceste (Alcestis), shown with the winged god of Love, commands the dreaming Chaucer to write *The Legend of Good Women* ("At Cleopatre I wol that thou beginne"). See also pp. 20, 46 &.130. In Tennyson's poem, Cleopatra speaks of her death as Antony's wife:

> *"The man, my lover, with whom I rode sublime*
> *On Fortune's neck: we sat as God by God:*
> *The Nilus would have risen before his time*
> *And flooded at our nod ….*
>
> *"I died a Queen. The Roman soldier found*
> *Me lying dead, my crown about my brows,*
> *A name for ever! – lying robed and crown'd,*
> *Worthy a Roman spouse."*

Two Middle English Versions

Middle English version 1 (Skeat)

After the deeth of Tholomee the king,
That al Egipte hadde in his governing,
Regned his quene Cleopataras[1];
Til on a tyme befel ther swiche a cas
That out of Rome was sent a senatour,
For to conqueren regnes and honour
Unto the toun of Rome, as was usaunce,
To have the world unto her obeisaunce[2];
And, sooth to seye, Antonius was his name.
So fil hit, as Fortune him oghte a shame
Whan he was fallen in prosperitee,
Rebel unto the toun of Rome is he.
And over al this, the suster of Cesar,
He lafte her falsly, er that she was war,
And wolde algates han another wyf;
For whiche he took with Rome and Cesar stryf.
  Natheles, for-sooth, this ilke senatour
Was a ful worthy gentil werreyour,
And of his deeth hit was ful greet damage.
But love had broght this man in swiche a rage,
And him so narwe bounden in his las,
Al for the love of Cleopataras[1],

Chaucer's *The Legend of Cleopatra*

That al the world he sette at no value.
Him thoughte, nas to him no thing so due
As Cleopatras for to love and serve;
Him roghte nat in armes for to sterve
In the defence of her, and of her right.
    This noble quene eek lovede so this knight,
Through his desert, and for his chivalrye;
As certeinly, but-if that bokes lye,
He was, of persone and of gentilesse,
And of discrecioun and hardinesse,
Worthy to any wight that liven may.
And she was fair as is the rose in May.
And, for to maken shortly is the beste,
She wex his wyf, and hadde him as her leste.
    The wedding and the feste to devyse,
To me, that have y-take swiche empryse
Of so many a story for to make,
Hit were to long, lest that I sholde slake
Of thing that bereth more effect and charge;
For men may overlade a ship or barge;
And forthy to theffect than wol I skippe,
And al the remenant, I wol lete hit slippe.
    Octovian, that wood was of this dede,
Shoop him an ost on Antony to lede
Al-outerly for his destruccioun,
With stoute Romains, cruel as leoun;

Two Middle English Versions

To ship they wente, and thus I let hem saile.
    Antonius was war, and wol nat faile
To meten with thise Romains, if he may;
Took eek his reed, and bothe, upon a day,
His wyf and he, and al his ost, forth wente
To shippe anoon, no lenger they ne stente;
And in the see hit happed hem to mete –
Up goth the trompe – and for to shoute and shete,
And peynen hem to sette on with the sonne.
With grisly soun out goth the grete gonne,
And heterly they hurtlen al at ones,
And fro the top doun cometh the grete stones.
In goth the grapenel so ful of crokes
Among the ropes, and the shering-hokes.
In with the polax presseth he and he;
Behynd the mast beginneth he to flee,
And out agayn, and dryveth him over-borde;
He stingeth him upon his speres orde;
He rent the sail with hokes lyke a sythe;
He bringeth the cuppe, and biddeth hem be blythe;
He poureth pesen upon the hacches slider;
With pottes ful of lym they goon to-gider;
And thus the longe day in fight they spende
Til, at the laste, as every thing hath ende,
Anthony is shent, and put him to the flighte,
And al his folk to-go, that best go mighte.

Chaucer's *The Legend of Cleopatra*

 Fleeth eek the queen, with al her purpre sail,
For strokes, which that wente as thikke as hail;
No wonder was, she mighte hit nat endure.
And whan that Anthony saw that aventure,
"Allas!" quod he, "the day that I was born!
My worshipe in this day thus have I lorn!"
And for dispeyr out of his witte he sterte,
And roof him-self anoon through-out the herte
Er that he ferther wente out of the place.
His wyf, that coude of Cesar have no grace,
To Egipte is fled, for drede and for distresse;
But herkneth, ye that speke of kyndenesse.

 Ye men, that falsly sweren many an oth
That ye wol dye, if that your love be wroth,
Heer may ye seen of women whiche a trouthe!
This woful Cleopatre hath mad swich routhe
That ther nis tonge noon that may hit telle.
But on the morwe she wol no lenger dwelle,
But made her subtil werkmen make a shryne
Of alle the rubies and the stones fine
In al Egipte that she coude espye;
And putte ful the shryne of spycerye,
And leet the cors embaume; and forth she fette
This dede cors, and in the shryne hit shette.
And next the shryne a pit than doth she grave;
And alle the serpents that she mighte have,

Two Middle English Versions

She putte hem in that grave, and thus she seyde:
"Now, love, to whom my sorweful herte obeyede
So ferforthly that, fro that blisful houre
That I yow swor to been al frely youre,
I mene yow, Antonius my knight!
That never waking, in the day or night,
Ye nere out of myn hertes remembraunce
For wele or wo, for carole or for daunce;
And in my-self this covenant made I tho,
That, right swich as ye felten, wele or wo,
As ferforth as hit in my power lay,
Unreprovable unto my wyfhood ay,
The same wolde I felen, lyf or deeth.
And thilke covenant, whyl me lasteth breeth,
I wol fulfille, and that shal wel be sene;
Was never unto her love a trewer quene."
And with that word, naked, with ful good herte,
Among the serpents in the pit she sterte,
And ther she chees to han her buryinge.
Anoon the neddres gonne her for to stinge,
And she her deeth receyveth, with good chere,
For love of Antony, that was her so dere; –
And this is storial sooth, hit is no fable.
    Now, er I fynde a man thus trewe and stable,
And wol for love his deeth so frely take,
I pray god lat our hedes never ake! [3]

Chaucer's *The Legend of Cleopatra*

La Morte di Marco Antonio (The Death of Mark Antony)
Pompeo Girolamo Batoni, 1763
© *Musée des Beaux-Arts de Brest, France/Bridgeman Images*

Although in Chaucer's *The Legend of Cleopatra*, Antony kills himself shortly after seeing Cleopatra fleeing the Battle of Actium – a detail which accords with the authors of Chaucer's two most likely sources, Annæus Florus and Vincent de Beauvais (see Appendices I and II) – the usual account, as depicted in Batoni's painting, is that Antony died in Cleopatra's arms before she too committed suicide. The emotional intensity of the painting is conveyed by the way in which the lovers gaze into each other's eyes, and in the tenderness with which they place their hands upon each other. It is curious that Chaucer, though he was surely aware of this more emotionally-charged, and certainly more romantic, version of the lovers' deaths, decided to omit it from his poem, whilst he nevertheless dwelt at some length upon the depth of Cleopatra's feeling for Antony. Pehaps this is further evidence that Chaucer wished to tell the story as briefly as possible. (See also pp. 130–135 and 170.)

Two Middle English Versions

Middle English version 2 (Robinson)

After the deth of Tholome the kyng,
That al Egipt hadde in his governyng,
Regned his queene Cleopataras[1];
Tyl on a tyme befel ther swich a cas
That out of Rome was sent a senatour,
For to conqueren regnes and honour
Unto the toun of Rome, as was usaunce,
To han the world at hire obeÿsaunce[2];
And, soth to seyne, Antonius was his name.
So fil it, as Fortune hym oughte a shame
Whan he was fallen in prosperite,
Rebel unto the toun of Rome is he.
And over al this, the suster of Cesar,
He lafte hire falsly, or that she was war,
And wolde algates han another wyf;
For which he tok with Rome and Cesar stryf.
Natheles, for-sothe, this ilke senatour
Was a ful worthy gentil werreyour,
And of his deth hit was ful gret damage.
But love hadde brought this man in swich a rage,
And hym so narwe bounden in his las,
Al for the love of Cleopataras[1],

That al the world he sette at no value.
Hym thoughte there nas nothyng to hym so due
As Cleopatras for to love and serve;
Him roughte nat in armes for to sterve
In the defence of hyre, and of hire ryght.
This noble quene ek lovede so this knyght,
Thourgh his desert, and for his chyvalrye;
As certeynly, but if that bokes lye,
He was, of persone and of gentillesse,
And of discrecioun and hardynesse,
Worthi to any wyght that liven may.
And she was fayr as is the rose in May.
And, for to make shortly is the beste,
She wex his wif, and hadde hym as hire leste.

    The weddynge and the feste to devyse,
To me, that have ytake swich empryse
Of so many a story for to make,
It were to longe, lest that I shulde slake
Of thyng that bereth more effect and charge;
For men may overlade a ship or barge;
And forthy to th'effect thanne wol I skyppe,
And al the remenaunt, I wol lete it slippe.

    Octovyan, that wod was of this dede,
Shop hym an ost on Antony to lede
Al uterly for his destruccioun,
With stoute Romeyns, crewel as lyoun;

Two Middle English Versions

To ship they wente, and thus I lat hem sayle.
Antonius was war, and wol nat fayle
To meten with these Romeyns, if he may;
Tok ek his red, and bothe, upon a day,
His wif and he, and al his ost, forth wente
To shipe anon, no lengere they ne stente;
And in the se it happede hem to mete.
Up goth the trompe, and for to shoute and shete,
And peynen hem to sette on with the sunne.
With grysely soun out goth the grete gonne,
And heterly they hurtelen al atones,
And from the top doun come the grete stones.
In goth the grapenel so ful of crokes
Among the ropes renne the sherynge-hokes.
In with the polax presseth he and he;
Byhynde the mast begynnyth he to fle,
And out ageyn, and dryveth hym overbord;
He styngeth hym upon his speres ord;
He rent the seyl with hokes lyke a sithe;
He bryngeth the cuppe, and biddeth hem be blythe;
He poureth pesen upon the haches slidere;
With pottes ful of lyme they gon togidere;
And thus the longe day in fyght they spende
Tyl at the laste, as every thyng hath ende,
Antony is schent and put hym to the flyghte,
And al his folk to-go, that best go myghte.

Fleth ek the queen, with al hire purpre sayl,
For strokes, whiche that wente as thikke as hayl;
No wonder was she myghte it nat endure.
And whan that Antony saw that aventure,
"Allas," quod he, "the day that I was born!
My worshipe in this day thus have I lorn!"
And for dispeyr out of his wit he sterte,
And rof hymself anon thourghout the herte
Or that he ferther wente out of the place.
His wif, that coude of Cesar have no grace,
To Egipt is fled, for drede and for destresse;
But herkneth, ye that speken of kyndenesse.
Ye men, that falsly sweren many an oth
That ye wol deye if that youre love be wroth,
Here may ye sen of wemen which a trouthe!
This woful Cleopatre hath mad swich routhe
That ther is tonge non that may it telle.
But on the morwe she wolde no lengere dwelle,
But made hire subtyl werkmen make a shryne
Of alle the rubyes and the stones fine
In al Egypte that she coude espie;
And putte ful the shryne of spicerye,
And let the cors embaume; and forth she fette
This dede cors, and in the shryne it shette.
And next the shryne a pit thanne doth she grave;
And alle the serpentes that she myghte have,

Two Middle English Versions

She putte hem in that grave, and thus she seyde:
"Now, love, to whom my sorweful herte obeyede
So ferforthly that from that blisful houre
That I yow swor to ben al frely youre –
I mene yow, Antonius my knyght –
That never wakynge, in the day or nyght,
Ye nere out of myn hertes remembraunce
For wel or wo, for carole or for daunce;
And in myself this covenaunt made I tho,
That, ryght swich as ye felten, wel or wo,
As fer forth as it in my power lay,
Unreprovable unto my wyfhood ay,
The same wolde I fele, lyf or deth –
And thilke covenant whil me lasteth breth,
I wol fulfille; and that shal ben wel sene;
Was never unto hire love a trewer quene."
And with that word, naked, with ful good herte,
Among the serpents in the pit she sterte,
And there she ches to have hire buryinge.
Anon the nedderes gonne hire for to stynge,
And she hire deth receyveth, with good cheere,
For love of Antony that was hire so dere: –
And this is storyal soth, it is no fable.
Now, or I fynde a man thus trewe and stable,
And wol for love his deth so frely take,
I preye God lat oure hedes nevere ake![3]

Notes

1. The spelling Cleopat*aras* is a device to make the lines scan as iambic pentameters (see p. 102).

2. "obeÿsaunce" is changed to "obesaunce" in the 2008 *The Riverside Chaucer*.

3. Chaucer then adds "Amen." This is the only *Legend* in which this occurs (see Note 40, p. 88).

Alcestis and the Winged God of Love
Walter Crane, 1876
© *The Victoria & Albert Museum, London*

See the illustration on p. 34 which also depicts Alcestis (Alceste) accompanied by the god of Love (see also p. 130).

4

Comparison and Literal Translation of the Middle English Versions

Line-by-line comparison

There now follows a detailed comparison of Skeat's 1889 version (Middle English version 1) with the 1933 version presented by Robinson (Middle English version 2), which latter also appears in the third edition of *The Riverside Chaucer* (Benson, 2008), with, as noted in the previous chapter, a slight change of spelling in only one word.

Each of the following paragraphs contains: (1) the Middle English text after Skeat (1889), preceded by the symbol (**S**); (2) the Middle English text after Robinson (1933), preceded by (**R**); (3) a literal translation of these versions into Modern English (in *italics*); and finally (4) a reorganized or rephrased Modern English version (in a Century Gothic typeface). Where differences in spelling, and occasionally in punctuation, occur between Middle English Versions 1 (**S**) and 2 (**R**), these are indicated by underlining.

Superscripts relate to notes which explain, or enlarge upon, particular words or phrases. A glossary appears in Chapter 5.

Chaucer's *The Legend of Cleopatra*

S: After the <u>deeth</u> of <u>Tholomee</u> the <u>king</u>,
R: After the <u>deth</u> of <u>Tholome</u> the <u>kyng</u>,
After the death of Ptolemy the king
After the death of Ptolemy[1], the king

S: That al <u>Egipte</u> hadde in his <u>governing</u>,
R: That al <u>Egipt</u> hadde in his <u>governyng</u>,
That all Egypt had in his governing
Who ruled over all Egypt,

S: Regned his <u>quene</u> Cleopataras;
R: Regned his <u>queene</u> Cleopataras;
Reigned his queen Cleopatra;
His queen, Cleopatra, reigned

S: <u>Til</u> on a tyme befel ther <u>swiche</u> a cas
R: <u>Tyl</u> on a tyme befel ther <u>swich</u> a cas
Til on a time befell there such an event
Until a time came[2] when it happened

S: That out of Rome was sent a senatour,
R: That out of Rome was sent a senatour,
That out of Rome was sent a senator
That a senator[3] was sent from Rome

S: For to conqueren regnes and honour
R: For to conqueren regnes and honour
For to conquer kingdoms and honour
To conquer kingdoms, and win honour

Comparison and Literal Translation of the Middle English Versions

S: Unto the toun of Rome, as was usaunce,
R: Unto the toun of Rome, as was usaunce,
Unto the town of Rome, as was custom
For Rome, as its custom was

S: To <u>have</u> the world <u>unto</u> <u>her</u> obeisaunce;
R: To <u>han</u> the world <u>at</u> <u>hire</u> obeÿsaunce;
To have the world at her obedience;
To bring the world under its control;

S: And, <u>sooth</u> to <u>seye</u>, Antonius was his name.
R: And, <u>soth</u> to <u>seyne</u>, Antonius was his name.
And truth to tell, Antonius was his name.
And, in truth, his name was Antony.

S: So fil <u>hit</u>, as Fortune <u>him</u> <u>oghte</u> a shame
R: So fil <u>it</u>, as Fortune <u>hym</u> <u>oughte</u> a shame
So befell it, as Fortune him owed a shame
It so happened that, as Fortune owed him disgrace[4]

S: Whan he was fallen in <u>prosperitee</u>,
R: Whan he was fallen in <u>prosperite</u>,
When he was fallen in prosperity,
Because he had been successful,

S: Rebel unto the toun of Rome is he.
R: Rebel unto the toun of Rome is he.
Rebel unto the town of Rome is he.
He was seen as rebelling[5] against Rome.

S: And over al this, the suster of Cesar,
R: And over al this, the suster of Cesar,
And over all this, the sister of Caesar,
And, moreover, Caesar's[6] sister[7]

S: He lafte <u>her</u> falsly, <u>er</u> that she was war,
R: He lafte <u>hire</u> falsly, <u>or</u> that she was war,
He left her falsely, ere that she was aware,
He had disloyally deserted, before she realized it[8],

S: And wolde algates han another wyf;
R: And wolde algates han another wyf;
And wished always to have another wife,
And always wished[9] to take a different wife.

S: For whiche he <u>took</u> with Rome and Cesar stryf.
R: For whiche he <u>tok</u> with Rome and Cesar stryf.
For which he took with Rome and Caesar strife.
And thus he quarrelled with both Rome and Caesar.

S: Natheles, for-<u>sooth</u>, this ilke senatour
R: Natheles, for-<u>sothe</u>, this ilke senatour
Nevertheless, for truth, this same senator
Nevertheless, in truth, this same senator

S: Was a ful worthy gentil werreyour,
R: Was a ful worthy gentil werreyour,
Was a full worthy noble warrior,
Was a very worthy, noble soldier.

Comparison and Literal Translation of the Middle English Versions

S: And of his <u>deeth</u> <u>hit</u> was ful <u>greet</u> damage.
R: And of his <u>deth</u> <u>it</u> was ful <u>gret</u> damage.
And of his death it was full great sadness.
And his death was met with great sadness.

S: But love <u>had</u> <u>broght</u> this man in <u>swiche</u> a rage,
R: But love <u>hadde</u> <u>brought</u> this man in <u>swich</u> a rage,
But love had brought this man in such a rage,
But love had made this man so foolhardy,

S: And <u>him</u> so narwe bounden in his las,
R: And <u>hym</u> so narwe bounden in his las,
And him so narrowly bound in its snare,
And had bound him so tightly in its snare,

S: Al for the love of Cleopataras,
R: Al for the love of Cleopataras,
All for the love of Cleopatra,
All for the love of Cleopatra,

S: That al the world he sette at no value.
R: That al the world he sette at no value.
That all the world he set at no value.
That all the world he set at no value.

S: <u>Him</u> thoughte, nas to <u>him</u> <u>no thing</u> so due
R: <u>Hym</u> thoughte <u>there</u> nas <u>nothyng</u> to hym so due
He thought there was nothing to him so needed
He thought nothing so needful to him

51

Chaucer's *The Legend of Cleopatra*

S: As Cleopatras for to love and serve;
R: As Cleopatras for to love and serve;
As Cleopatra for to love and serve;
As loving and serving Cleopatra;

S: Him roghte nat in armes for to sterve
R: Hym roughte nat in armes for to sterve
He cared not in arms for to die
He did not care if he died in battle

S: In the defence of her, and of her right.
R: In the defence of hyre, and of hire ryght.
In the defence of her, and of her right.
In defence of her and of her right[10].

S: This noble quene eek lovede so this knight,
R: This noble quene ek lovede so this knyght,
This noble queen likewise loved so this knight,
This noble queen likewise greatly loved this knight[11],

S: Through his desert, and for his chivalrye;
R: Thourgh his desert, and for his chyvalrye;
Through his merit, and for his chivalry;
For his qualities and for his chivalry;

S: As certeinly, but-if that bokes lye,
R: As certeynly, but if that bokes lye,
As certainly, unless that books lie,
Certainly, unless books[12] lie,

52

Comparison and Literal Translation of the Middle English Versions

S: He was, of persone and of <u>gentilesse</u>,
R: He was, of persone and of <u>gentillesse</u>,
He was, of person and of nobility
He was, in personality[13] and nobility

S: And of discrecioun and <u>hardinesse</u>,
R: And of discrecioun and <u>hardynesse</u>,
And of discretion and hardiness,
And soundness of judgement[14] and strength,

S: <u>Worthy</u> to any <u>wight</u> that liven may.
R: <u>Worthi</u> to any <u>wyght</u> that liven may.
Worthy to any creature that live may.
As worthy as any living man.

S: And she was fair as is the rose in May.
R: And she was <u>fayr</u> as is the rose in May.
And she was fair as is the rose in May.
And she was as fair as the rose in May.

S: And, for to <u>maken</u> shortly is the beste,
R: And, for to <u>make</u> shortly is the beste,
And, for to make shortly is the best,
And (for it is best to tell it briefly)

S: She wex his <u>wyf</u>, and hadde <u>him</u> as <u>her</u> leste.
R: She wex his <u>wif</u>, and hadde <u>hym</u> as <u>hire</u> leste.
She became his wife, and had him as her pleasure.
She became his wife, and had him as she desired[15].

Chaucer's *The Legend of Cleopatra*

Cleopatra on the Terraces of Philae (detail)
Frederick Arthur Bridgman, 1896
© *Dahesh Museum of Art, New York*

"And she was fair as is the rose in May." Bridgman's painting shows Cleopatra preparing to leave the island of Philae which was then regarded as holy, being the supposed burial place of Isis (whose reincarnation Cleopatra claimed to be). It is said that during their time together in Alexandria, Cleopatra would dress as Isis and Antony as Osiris (the husband of Isis), though this is not mentioned in Chaucer's poem. Cleopatra is shown here in dress that is somewhat more Egyptian in style than depicted by many earlier artists. In the top left of the picture is the Kiosk of Trajan – an anachronism, because this structure actually postdated Cleopatra by more than a century.

Comparison and Literal Translation of the Middle English Versions

S: The <u>wedding</u> and the feste to devyse,
R: The <u>weddynge</u> and the feste to devyse,
The wedding and the feast to describe,
To describe the wedding and the feast,

S: To me, that have <u>y-take</u> <u>swiche</u> emprise
R: To me, that have <u>ytake</u> <u>swich</u> empryse
To me, that has undertaken such an enterprise
To me, who has undertaken the task

S: Of so many a story for to make,
R: Of so many a story for to make,
Of so many a story for to make,
Of telling so many stories,

S: <u>Hit</u> were to <u>long</u>, lest that I <u>sholde</u> slake
R: <u>It</u> were to <u>longe</u>, lest that I <u>shulde</u> slake
It were too long, lest that I should diminish
Would take too long[16], in case I should understate

S: Of <u>thing</u> that bereth more effect and charge;
R: Of <u>thyng</u> that bereth more effect and charge;
Of something that bears more effect and load;
Things of more importance and significance;

S: For men may overlade a ship or barge;
R: For men may overlade a ship or barge;
For men may overload a ship or barge;
For men may overload a ship or barge;

S: And forthy to theffect than wol I skippe,
R: And forthy to th'effect thanne wol I skyppe,
  And therefore to the main point then will I skip,
  And I will therefore skip to the important matters,

S: And al the remenant, I wol lete hit slippe.
R: And al the remenaunt, I wol lete it slippe.
  And all the remainder, I will let it slip.
  And I will drop the rest.

S: Octovian, that wood was of this dede,
R: Octovyan, that wod was of this dede,
  Octavian, that maddened was of this deed,
  Octavian, who was enraged by this deed[17],

S: Shoop him an ost on Antony to lede
R: Shop hym an ost on Antony to lede
  Raised himself an host on Antony to lead
  Raised an army to lead against Antony,

S: Al-outerly for his destruccioun,
R: Al uterly for his destruccioun,
  Utterly for his destruction,
  Solely for his destruction,

S: With stoute Romains, cruel as leoun;
R: With stoute Romeyns, crewel as lyoun;
  With stout Romans, cruel as lions;
  With stout Romans, cruel as lions;

Comparison and Literal Translation of the Middle English Versions

S: To ship they wente, and thus I <u>let</u> hem <u>saile</u>.
R: To ship they wente, and thus I <u>lat</u> hem <u>sayle</u>.
To ship they went, and thus I let them sail.
They went to their ships, and I leave them thus, setting sail.

S: Antonius was war, and wol nat <u>faile</u>
R: Antonius was war, and wol nat <u>fayle</u>
Antonius was aware, and will not fail
Antony knew of this, and did not wish to avoid

S: To meten with <u>thise</u> <u>Romains</u>, if he may;
R: To meten with <u>these</u> <u>Romeyns</u>, if he may;
To meet with these Romans, if he may;
Engaging with these Romans, if he could.[18]

S: Took <u>eek</u> his <u>reed</u>, and bothe, upon a day,
R: Tok <u>ek</u> his <u>red</u>, and bothe, upon a day,
He took also his own counsel, and both, upon a day,
He also made his plans, and one day both

S: His <u>wyf</u> and he, and al his ost, forth wente
R: His <u>wif</u> and he, and al his ost, forth wente
His wife and he, and all his host, forth went
His wife and he, and all his men, went

S: To <u>shippe</u> <u>anoon</u>, no <u>lenger</u> they ne stente;
R: To <u>shipe</u> <u>anon</u>, no <u>lengere</u> they ne stente;
To ships anon, no longer they did not wait;
To their ships straight away, waiting no longer;

S: And in the <u>see</u> <u>hit</u> <u>happed</u> hem to <u>mete</u> –
R: And in the <u>se</u> <u>it</u> <u>happede</u> hem to <u>mete.</u>
And in the sea it happened them to meet –
And at sea they met.

S: Up goth the trompe – and for to shoute and shete,
R: Up goth the trompe – and for to shoute and shete,
Up goes the trumpet – and for to shout and shoot,
The trumpet[19] sounds – and shouting and shooting[20],

S: And peynen hem to sette on with the sonne.
R: And peynen hem to sette on with the sonne.
And taking pains to look with the sun.
And they take care to keep their backs to the sun.[21]

S: With <u>grisly</u> soun out goth the grete gonne,
R: With <u>grisely</u> soun out goth the grete gonne,
With a grisly sound out goes the great gun,
With a terrible sound the great gun[22] fires,

S: And heterly they <u>hurtlen</u> al <u>at ones</u>,
R: And heterly they <u>hurtelen</u> al <u>atones</u>,
And fiercely they hurl all at each other
And fiercely they attack each other

S: And <u>fro</u> the top doun <u>cometh</u> the grete stones.
R: And <u>from</u> the top doun <u>come</u> the grete stones.
And from the top down come the great stones.
And from above fall the great stones.

Comparison and Literal Translation of the Middle English Versions

S: In goth the grapenel so ful of crokes
R: In goth the grapenel so ful of crokes
In go the grapnels so full of claws
In go the grapnels[23] so full of claws[24]

S: Among the ropes, <u>and</u> the <u>shering</u>-hokes.
R: Among the ropes, <u>renne</u> the <u>sherynge</u>-hokes.
*Among the ropes, and(**S**)/run(**R**) the shear-hooks.*
Among the ropes, and in run the shear-hooks[25] too.

S: In with the polax presseth he and he;
R: In with the polax presseth he and he;
In with the polaxe presses he and he;
One man with a battle-axe pushes against another,

S: <u>Behynd</u> the mast <u>beginneth</u> he to <u>flee</u>,
R: <u>Byhynde</u> the mast <u>begynnyth</u> he to <u>fle</u>,
Behind the mast begins he to flee,
Who starts to run behind the mast,

S: And out agayn, and dryveth <u>him</u> <u>over-borde</u>;
R: And out ageyn, and dryveth <u>hym</u> <u>overbord</u>;
And out again, and drives him overboard;
And then out again, driving the other man overboard;[26]

S: He <u>stingeth</u> <u>him</u> upon his speres <u>orde</u>;
R: He <u>styngeth</u> <u>hym</u> upon his speres <u>ord</u>;
One stings him upon his spear's point;
One man stabs himself[27] on the point of his spear;

59

Chaucer's *The Legend of Cleopatra*

S: He rent the sail with hokes lyke a sythe;
R: He rent the seyl with hokes lyke a sithe;
He rends the sail with hooks lyke a sythe;
One slashes the sail with scythe-like hooks;

S: He bringeth the cuppe, and biddeth hem be blythe;
R: He bryngeth the cuppe, and biddeth hem be blythe;
He brings the cup, and bids them be blithe;
One[28] holds a goblet, and bids them all be cheerful;

S: He poureth pesen upon the hacches slider;
R: He poureth pesen upon the haches slidere;
He pours peas upon the hatches slippery;
One pours peas on the hatches,[29] making them slippery;

S: With pottes ful of lym they goon to-gider;
R: With pottes ful of lyme they gon togidere;
With pots full of lime they go together;
Bearing pots full of quicklime, they rush at each other;

S: And thus the longe day in fight they spende
R: And thus the longe day in fyght they spende
And thus the long day in fight they spend
And thus they spend the long day in battle

S: Til, at the laste, as every thing hath ende,
R: Tyl at the laste, as every thyng hath ende,
Til, at the last, as everything has end,
Until, at last – as all things must come to an end –

60

Comparison and Literal Translation of the Middle English Versions

S: Antony is <u>shent</u>, and put <u>him</u> to the <u>flighte</u>,
R: Antony is <u>schent</u> and put <u>hym</u> to the <u>flyghte</u>,
Antony is destroyed, and put him to the flight,
Antony is beaten, and put to flight,

S: And al his folk to-go, that best go <u>mighte</u>.
R: And al his folk to-go, that best go <u>myghte</u>.
And all his folk scatter, that best go might.
And all his men escape as best they can.

S: Fleeth <u>eek</u> the queen, with al <u>her</u> purpre <u>sail</u>,
R: Fleth <u>ek</u> the queen, with al <u>hire</u> purpre <u>sayl</u>,
Flees similarly the queen, with all her purple sail,
So too flees the queen, with her purple[30] sails,

S: For strokes, <u>which</u> that wente as thikke as <u>hail</u>;
R: For strokes, <u>whiche</u> that wente as thikke as <u>hayl</u>;
For strokes, which went as thick as hail;
From the missiles which fell as thick as hail;

S: No wonder was, she <u>mighte hit</u> nat endure.
R: No wonder was she <u>myghte it</u> nat endure.
No wonder was, she might it not endure.
It was no wonder that she could not endure it.

S: And whan that Antony saw that aventure,
R: And whan that Antony saw that aventure,
And what that Antony saw that about to happen,
And when Antony saw that chance[31] being taken,

61

Chaucer's *The Legend of Cleopatra*

Cleopatra's Galley at the Battle of Actium
Warwick Goble, 1912

From a colour illustration in The Modern Reader's Chaucer:
The Complete Poetical Works of Geoffrey Chaucer
by J. S. P. Tatlock (1912). Image © Marius Press.

"Fleeth eek the queen, with al her purpre sail." The erroneous notion that Cleopatra's ship at Actium bore purple sails (see: p. 84; pp. 85 & 86; Chapter 9; and Appendices) is perpetuated even into the 20th century in this fanciful illustration.

Comparison and Literal Translation of the Middle English Versions

S: "Allas!" quod he, "the day that I was born!
R: "Allas," quod he, "the day that I was born!
"Alas!" said he, "the day that I was born!
"I rue," he said, "the day that I was born!

S: My worshipe in this day thus have I lorn!"
R: My worshipe in this day thus have I lorn."
My worship in this day thus have I lost!"
This day I have lost my honour!"

S: And for dispeyr out of his <u>witte</u> he sterte,
R: And for dispeyr out of his <u>wit</u> he sterte,
And for despair out of his wits he started,
And despair drove him out of his mind,

S: And <u>roof</u> <u>him-self</u> <u>anoon</u> <u>through-out</u> the herte
R: And <u>rof</u> <u>hymself</u> <u>anon</u> <u>thourghout</u> the herte
And stabbed himself anon throughout the heart
And he at once stabbed himself through the heart

S: <u>Er</u> that he ferther wente out of the place.
R: <u>Or</u> that he ferther wente out of the place.
Ere that he further went out of the place.
Before he went out of the place of battle[32].

S: His <u>wyf</u>, that coude of Cesar have no grace,
R: His <u>wif</u>, that coude of Cesar have no grace,
His wife, that could of Caesar have no grace,
His wife, who could expect no mercy from Caesar,

63

Chaucer's *The Legend of Cleopatra*

S: To <u>Egipte</u> is fled, for drede and for <u>distresse</u>;
R: To <u>Egipt</u> is fled, for drede and for <u>destresse</u>;
To Egypt is fled, for dread and for distress;
Fled to Egypt, in fear and distress;

S: But herkneth, ye that <u>speke</u> of kyndenesse.
R: But herkneth, ye that <u>speken</u> of kyndenesse.
But hearken, you that speak of kindness.
But listen, all you who speak of love.

S: Ye men, that falsly sweren many an oth
R: Ye men, that falsly sweren many an oth
You men, that falsely swear many an oath
You men, who falsely swear many an oath

S: That ye wol <u>dye</u>, if that <u>your</u> love be wroth,
R: That ye wol <u>deye</u> if that <u>youre</u> love be wroth,
That you will die, if that your love be angered,
That you will die if your loved one should be angered,

S: <u>Heer</u> may ye <u>seen</u> of <u>women</u> <u>whiche</u> a trouthe!
R: <u>Here</u> may ye <u>sen</u> of <u>wemen</u> <u>which</u> a trouthe!
Here may you see of a woman such a truth!
Here you can see truthfulness in a woman!

S: This woful Cleopatre hath mad swich routhe
R: This woful Cleopatre hath mad swich routhe
This woeful Cleopatra has made such lamentation
The disconsolate Cleopatra grieved so much

Comparison and Literal Translation of the Middle English Versions

S: That ther <u>nis</u> tonge <u>noon</u> that may <u>hit</u> telle.
R: That ther <u>is</u> tonge <u>non</u> that may <u>it</u> telle.
That there is not tongue that may it tell.
There is no language which can describe it.

S: But on the morwe she <u>wol</u> no <u>lenger</u> dwelle,
R: But on the morwe she <u>wolde</u> no <u>lengere</u> dwelle,
But on the morrow she wishes no longer dwell,
But the following morning she wished to delay no longer

S: But made <u>her</u> <u>subtil</u> werkmen make a shryne
R: But made <u>hire</u> <u>subtyl</u> werkmen make a shryne
But made her subtle workmen make a shrine
But commanded her skilled craftsmen to build a shrine

S: Of alle the <u>rubies</u> and the stones <u>fine</u>
R: Of alle the <u>rubyes</u> and the stones <u>fyne</u>
Of all the rubies and the stones fine
Of all the rubies and fine gemstones

S: In al <u>Egipte</u> that she coude <u>espye</u>;
R: In al <u>Egypte</u> that she coude <u>espie</u>;
In all Egypt that she could espy;
That she could find in the whole of Egypt;

S: And putte ful the shryne of <u>spycerye</u>,
R: And putte ful the shryne of <u>spicerye</u>,
And put full the shrine of spices,
And she filled the shrine with spices,

Chaucer's *The Legend of Cleopatra*

S: And <u>leet</u> the cors embaume; and forth she fette
R: And <u>let</u> the cors embaume; and forth she fette
And let the body embalm; and forth she fetched
And had the body embalmed[33]; and she fetched

S: This dede cors, and in the shryne <u>hit</u> shette.
R: This dede cors, and in the shryne <u>it</u> shette.
This dead corpse, and in the shrine it shut.
This dead body, and shut it in the shrine.

S: And next the shryne a pit <u>than</u> doth she grave;
R: And next the shryne a pit <u>thanne</u> doth she grave;
And next the shrine a pit then does she dig;
And beside the shrine[34] she then dug a pit;

S: And alle the <u>serpents</u> that she <u>mighte</u> have,
R: And alle the <u>serpentes</u> that she <u>myghte</u> have,
And all the serpents that she might have,
And all the snakes[35] that she could obtain,

S: She putte hem in that grave, and thus she seyde:
R: She putte hem in that grave, and thus she seyde:
She put them in that grave, and thus she said:
She put in that pit, and spoke thus[36]:

S: "Now, love, to whom my sorweful herte obeyede
R: "Now, love, to whom my sorweful herte obeyede
"Now, love, to whom my sorrowful heart obeyed
"Now, my beloved, whom my sorrowful heart obeyed

Comparison and Literal Translation of the Middle English Versions

S: So ferforthly that, <u>fro</u> that blisful houre
R: So ferforthly that <u>from</u> that blisful houre
So completely that, from that blissful hour
So completely that, from that blissful hour

S: That I yow swor to <u>been</u> al frely <u>youre</u> –
R: That I yow swor to <u>ben</u> al frely <u>youre,</u>
That I you swore to be all freely yours,
That I swore to you that I would willingly be yours –

S: I mene yow, Antonius my <u>knight</u>!
R: I mene yow, Antonius my <u>knyght</u> –
I mean you, Antonius my knight!
I mean you, Antony my knight! –

S: That never <u>waking</u>, in the day or <u>night</u>,
R: That never <u>wakynge</u>, in the day or <u>nyght</u>,
That never waking, in the day or night,
That never whilst awake, in the day or night,

S: Ye nere out of myn hertes remembraunce
R: Ye nere out of myn hertes remembraunce
You never out of my heart's remembrance
Were you ever out of my heart's memory

S: For <u>wele</u> or wo, for carole or for daunce;
R: For <u>wel</u> or wo, for carole or for daunce;
For happiness or woe, for carol or for dance,
In happiness or in sorrow, in song or in dance[37],

Chaucer's *The Legend of Cleopatra*

S: And in <u>my-self</u> this <u>covenant</u> made I tho,
R: And in <u>myself</u> this <u>covenaunt</u> made I tho,
And in myself this covenant made I then,
And I then made this pledge to myself

S: That, <u>right</u> swich as ye felten, <u>wele</u> or wo,
R: That, <u>ryght</u> swich as ye felten, <u>wel</u> or wo,
That, right such as you felt, well or woe,
That whatever you were to feel, happiness or sorrow,

S: As <u>ferforth</u> as <u>hit</u> in my power lay,
R: As <u>fer forth</u> as <u>it</u> in my power lay,
As much as it in my power lay,
Inasmuch as it lay in my power[38],

S: Unreprovable unto my wyfhood ay,
R: Unreprovable unto my wyfhood ay,
Irreproachable unto my wifehood ever,
Ever faithful to my wifely duty,

S: The same wolde I <u>felen</u>, lyf or <u>deeth</u>.
R: The same wolde I <u>fele</u>, lyf or <u>deth</u> –
The same wished I to feel, life or death.
I wished to feel the same, in life or death.

S: And thilke <u>covenant, whyl</u> me lasteth <u>breeth</u>,
R: And thilke <u>covenant whil</u> me lasteth <u>breth</u>,
And that very covenant, while me there lasts breath,
And, while I still draw breath, that very pledge

Comparison and Literal Translation of the Middle English Versions

S: I wol fulfille, and that shal <u>wel be</u> sene;
R: I wol fulfille; and that shal <u>ben wel</u> sene;
I will fulfil, and that shall well be seen;
I shall fulfil, and that shall be clearly seen;

S: Was never unto <u>her</u> love a trewer quene."
R: Was never unto <u>hire</u> love a trewer quene."
Was never unto her love a truer queen."
Never was there a queen truer to her loved one."

S: And with that word, naked, with ful good herte,
R: And with that word, naked, with ful good herte,
And with that word, naked, and with full good heart,
And thus saying, naked[39], and with a cheerful heart,

S: Among the serpents in the pit she sterte,
R: Among the serpents in the pit she sterte,
Among the serpents in the pit she leaps,
She casts herself into the pit, among the snakes,

S: And <u>ther</u> she <u>chees</u> to <u>han</u> <u>her</u> buryinge.
R: And <u>there</u> she <u>ches</u> to <u>have</u> <u>hire</u> buryinge.
And there she chooses to have her burying.
And there she chooses to be buried.

S: <u>Anoon</u> the <u>neddres</u> gonne <u>her</u> for to <u>stinge</u>,
R: <u>Anon</u> the <u>nedderes</u> gonne <u>hire</u> for to <u>stynge</u>,
Immediately, the adders begin her for to sting,
The snakes immediately begin to sting her,

Chaucer's *The Legend of Cleopatra*

S: And she <u>her</u> <u>deeth</u> receyveth, with good <u>chere</u>,
R: And she <u>hire</u> <u>deth</u> receyveth, with good <u>cheere</u>,
And she her death receives, with good cheer,
And she receives her death cheerfully,

S: For love of Antony, that was <u>her</u> so dere;
R: For love of Antony that was <u>hire</u> so dere:
For love of Antony, that was her so dear:
For the love of Antony, who was so dear to her:

S: And this is <u>storial</u> <u>sooth</u>, <u>hit</u> is no fable.
R: And this is <u>storyal</u> <u>soth</u>, <u>it</u> is no fable.
And this is historical truth, it is no fable.
And this is historical fact; it is not a fable.

S: Now, <u>er</u> I fynde a man thus trewe and stable,
R: Now, <u>or</u> I fynde a man thus trewe and stable,
Now, until I find a man thus true and stable,
Now, until I find a man as true and constant as this,

S: And wol for love his <u>deeth</u> so frely take,
R: And wol for love his <u>deth</u> so frely take,
And will for love his death so freely take,
And who would so willingly die for his love,

S: I <u>pray</u> <u>god</u> lat <u>our</u> hedes <u>never</u> ake!
R: I <u>preye</u> <u>God</u> lat <u>oure</u> hedes <u>nevere</u> ake!
I pray God let our heads never ache!
I pray to God that our heads shall never ache! [40]

Comparison and Literal Translation of the Middle English Versions

Notes

1. ... the death of King Ptolemy

    Three kings bearing the name Ptolemy died during Cleopatra's lifetime: (i) Ptolemy XII Neos Dionysos (Ptolemy Auletes), Cleopatra's father, who died in 51 BC; (ii) Ptolemy XIII, the elder of Cleopatra's two younger brothers, and Cleopatra's husband and co-ruler of Egypt (drowned in 47 BC); and (iii) Ptolemy XIV, Cleopatra's younger brother and also her husband and (nominal) co-ruler of Egypt (he died, possibly murdered on Cleopatra's orders, in 44 BC). Although Cleopatra *became* a reigning queen after the death of her father Ptolemy XII (she was *already* queen at the deaths of both Ptolemy XIII and Ptolemy XIV), Chaucer's reference must be to Ptolemy XIV (or possibly Ptolemy XIII), because the phrase used is "his *queen*" and not "his *daughter*"; and "reigned" presumably implies "reigned *alone.*"

2. Until a time came ...

    The reference appears to be to the period after the Battle of Philippi (42 BC), when Antony undertook to remain in the East where he would attempt to bring the Eastern lands under Roman contol, while Octavian returned to Italy to resettle the veterans. Alhough it was at this time that Antony summoned

Cleopatra to Tarsus (see p. 73) to answer the charge that she had provided logistical support to Brutus and Cassius, Chaucer makes no reference to this, appearing to suggest that the liason between the two began with a visit by Antony to Egypt.

3.   ... a senator was sent from Rome

Antony was a member of the Roman senate when he joined Cleopatra in Egypt in 36 BC; he also held consular powers as one of the founder members of the Second Triumvirate which ruled Rome and its territories until its term expired in 33 BC.

4.   ... Fortune owed him disgrace

This is usually taken as meaning that Fate has a way of levelling all men – a rise in prosperity often being followed by misfortune. Chaucer is presumably making a reference to Fortuna, the Roman goddess of fortune, who was regarded as fickle and untrustworthy to the point of being vindictive.

5.   He was seen as rebelling against Rome

Or "was repudiated by Rome." Octavian attempted to raise his favourable profile in Rome by vilifying Antony for – amongst other things – his un-Roman habit of adopting, in the company of Cleopatra, the Hellenic style of dress worn by the Ptolemies.

Comparison and Literal Translation of the Middle English Versions

The Meeting of Antony and Cleopatra
Giovanni Battista Tiepolo, ca. 1747
© *The Scottish National Gallery*

"That out of Rome was sent a senatour." The meeting shown here was in Tarsus in 41 BC, though Chaucer appears to suggest that their liaison began later, in Alexandria in 36 BC (p. 71). Note how Cleopatra's dress transforms her from Egyptian queen to contemporary *femme fatale* (see p.147).

6. Caesar

   This refers to Octavian who, as the posthumously adopted son of Julius Caesar, and in accordance with Roman custom, assumed his adoptive father's name, Gaius Julius Caesar. He appended *divi filius* (son of a god) when Julius Caesar was later deified, but did not follow what would have been the usual practice of also adding "Octavianus" to indicate his pre-adoptive name.

7. Caesar's sister ...

   This was Octavian's younger sister Octavia, whom Antony had married to seal the Pact of Brundisium (40 BC). Fulvia, Antony's previous wife, had only recently died, as too had Marcellus, the husband of Octavia.

8. ... deserted, before she realized it

   Octavia could, in fact, hardly have been unaware of her husband's dalliance with Cleopatra; he had, after all, already had a very public affair with the Egyptian queen, which had commenced in Tarsus and was then continued in Alexandria, where he had fathered Cleopatra's twins Alexander Helios and Cleopatra Selene. Moreover, Octavia had been rejected by Antony after she delivered Octavian's message that the forty-thousand troops which had been promised to Antony by her brother Octavian would not, after all, be forthcoming. Perhaps less contentious interpretations would be "without her knowledge," or "without telling her."

9. And always wished …

In Middle English, "algate" ("algates" or "algatis" in different manuscripts) was used to mean "always," "in every case," "in any case," "at any rate," "all the same," "at all costs," "nevertheless," or "in every way." In the present context it is sometimes taken to imply "fervently," though it seems more likely that Chaucer's intention was to pass wry comment on Antony's lascivious nature by implying that he was "always" on the look-out for another wife (or, more accurately, mistress), though this particular aspect of Antony's nature is not referred to elsewhere in the poem.

10. … and of her right

It is not clear exactly to what Chaucer is referring here, though it is possible that it is to Cleopatra's desire to see the re-establishment of the Ptolemaic empire, which was then essentially under Roman domination, but which she regarded as rightfully hers. Antony did, indeed, seem to be determined to return the greater part of that empire to Cleopatra in the lavish ceremony later referred to as the Donations of Alexandria (34 BC); thus "hir right" could reasonably be interpreted as "her right to rule." Alternatively, one might take it simply to mean "her honour," and this would certainly be in accord with Chaucer's portrayal of Antony in this part of the poem as being courtly and chivalrous – knightly qualities which would be greatly admired by mediæval readers (see also Note 11, below).

11. ... greatly loved this knight

Here Chaucer uses the term "knight" to emphasize Antony's noble and chivalrous bearing, and not in reference to his position in Roman society, which at that time comprised three quite distinct classes of citizen, namely: the Aristocracy (to which Antony belonged); the Equites, who were also referred to as the Equestrian order or "knights"; and the rest of the people – the Plebeians. Schofield (1913) has suggested that by calling Antony a "knight," and by referring in this regard to both his "chivalrye" and his "gentilesse," Chaucer is giving mediæval colour to the story, thereby increasing its appeal to his contemporary audience. This same device, Schofield proposes, is employed by Chaucer in his dramatic description of the Battle of Actium (see p. 32 and Chapter 8).

12. ... unless books lie

Here, Chaucer is referring specifically to the history books.

13. He was in personality ...

The translation of "of persone" is difficult. Perhaps closest in Modern English is "personable," though "aimiable" might also be quite appropriate in this context. Jones (1971), however, has suggested that "in appearance" is better: i.e., Antony was "a fine figure of a man."

14. And of soundness of judgement ...

Antony is described as being "of discrecioun," and here what would be the closest modern rendering, i.e., "of discretion," seems hardly appropriate. The term has been translated in a number of ways, including: "wise," "sensitive," "thoughtful," "considerate," or "morally sound." To say that Antony was a man of "sound judgement," whilst it might reflect the way in which Cleopatra regarded him, certainly does not accord with what can only be described as his self-destructive behaviour at this point in his life. Following his defeat at Actium, for example, Antony appears simply to have accepted Octavian's supremacy, and thus his own inevitable fate, by failing to reassemble an army capable of defending

Alexandria (though all the vast resources of Egypt were at his disposal) and to have resigned himself instead to a life of idleness and pleasure.

15. ... and had him as she desired

Here, an alternative, and possibly more accurate, phrasing would be "and she possessed him at her pleasure." The implications of what appears to be a reference to Cleopatra's sexual desire have already been commented upon (see p. 26).

16. Would take too long ...

As elsewhere in *The Legend of Good Women*, it appears that here Chaucer is making an excuse to shorten the narrative. It has been suggested that, taking little interest in this project, he wished to get through it as quickly as possible. The fact that he did not complete *The Legend of Good Women* is also presented as evidence of his lack of commitment to the project. There are other explanations, however, some of which are considered in Chapter 7, where it is noted that whilst a digression into the details of Cleopatra's wedding and the subsequent feast would undeniably have impeded the progression of the storyline, Chaucer's subsequent extended justification for the omission has exactly the same effect (see pp. 132 & 133).

Comparison and Literal Translation of the Middle English Versions

17. ... enraged by this deed

    It is often assumed that the deed referred to is the wedding between Antony and Cleopatra, as this has been the subject of the immediately foregoing lines of the poem, though it has been proposed by some that Chaucer was actually alluding to the rejection by Antony of Octavian's sister Octavia.

18. ... did not wish to avoid ... engaging ... if he could

    Another interpretation might be: "... would not fail to engage ... if that proved necessary." As "faile" or "fayle" can also mean "be unsuccessful," another rendering might be "would be successful if he were able to engage with these Romans."

19. The trumpet sounds ...

    It is likely that any call given at the start of battle in Roman times would have been by the use of an instrument longer than a trumpet, and capable of a more sustained and far-reaching sound. Whilst it is likely that Chaucer did actually mean "trumpet" (see Chapter 8), it might be more in keeping with the age in which *The Legend of Cleopatra* is set if "trompe" were to be translated here as "horn."

20. ... and shooting

    Firearms would not, of course, have been used in the Battle of Actium, and it is probably accurate to regard "shete," translated as "shoot" or "shooting," as an anachronism (see pp. 141, 142, and 159). One may, however, "shoot" an arrow from a bow, or "fire" or "shoot" a missile from a catapult, and therefore, in order to maintain the image of a sea battle in Roman times, it has been suggested by some that it would be appropriate to translate this passage as referring to the launching of large stones and rocks (e.g., from deck-mounted wooden catapults).

21. ... they take care to keep their backs to the sun
Literally, "to observe, perceive, or set their eyes in the same direction as, the sun," i.e., to keep the sun out of their eyes, the better to see and thus avoid the falling rocks (see pp. 141 & 142).

22. With a terrible sound the great gun fires.
As with "shete" (shoot) – see Note 20, above – Chaucer's use of "gonne" (gun) has been referred to by some as anachronistic. However, Skeat (1889) denies this (see also p.142), and proposes that the word applied to any form of shot or missile, rather than to the instrument used to propel them; he quotes the use of "gonne," around the time of Chaucer's writing, to mean "missile." The "grisly soun," or "terrible sound," Skeat further suggests,

may allude to the "whizzing of the ponderous missile through the air," though Schofield (1913) has presented compelling arguments (detailed in Chapter 8) for the view that Chaucer was deliberately describing the type of naval engagement – including the use of cannons – which would have been familiar to his readers.

23. *In go the grapnels ...*

   A grapnel, or grappling-hook, was an iron device with multiple claws. Attached to a rope and thrown from a ship it would latch onto the side, decking or rigging of an enemy ship, enabling the two vessels to be pulled alongside each other, thus facilitating the process of boarding (see p. 143).

24. *... so full of claws*

   The "crokes" or "claws" are the hooks on the end of a grapnel (see Note 23, above, and p. 143).

25. *Among the ropes, and in run the shear-hooks*

   A shear-hook (shearing-hook), like a grapnel, was a metal device thrown from one ship to another, though with the primary intention not of drawing the two ships together but of slashing the other ship's rigging and sails, and thereby impeding or even totally incapacitating its manoeuverability (see p. 143).

26. One man with a battle-axe presses another,
    Who starts to run behind the mast,
    And then out again, driving the other man overboard;

    Skeat (1889) has described this short passage as "wonderfully graphic." Other writers have not been so generous. Quinn (1994), for example, refers to it as "irrelevant" and "overwrought" (p. 158). See also Schofield's interpretation (Chapter 9).

27. One man stabs himself ...

    The phrase "He stingeth him ..." could also be read as "One man stabs another ...," and indeeed both interpretations make perfect sense. The reflexive "stabs himself" would certainly be in accord with Chaucer's tendency to introduce an element of humour into even the most serious of passages.

28. One holds a goblet, and bids them all be cheerful

    Chaucer employs "he" repeatedly in his account of the battle of Actium, leading Quinn (1994) to speak of "an excited confusion of pronoun references," and indeed "he" is used to mean "one man" or "another man," as in "In with the polax presseth he and he," or, on other occasions, "this man" or "that man." It has sometimes been suggested that "He" in "He bringeth the cuppe, and biddeth hem be blythe," refers to Antony: thus Quinn (1994) speaks of "Antony's toast," and quotes others as assuming this to be the same cup out of which Antony then pours peas (see Note 29, below). Apart, though, from Antony's well-documented liking of wine (and reportedly to excess) there would appear to be little justification for linking Antony to the act of raising a cup to the fighting men, much less to that of the pouring of peas onto the deck. See also the point made by Schofield (1913) (p. 144).

29. One pours peas on the hatches ...

The use of dried peas or perhaps small pebbles to make a ship's deck slippery for those attempting to board may, according to some scholars, have been documented in Chaucer's time, though there is no recorded instance of such a device ever being used by the Romans. In any event, one wonders whether the procedure, if it had indeed ever been adopted, would not have had a similarly unbalancing effect upon those defending the invaded ship. It has even been suggested by some that it was Antony who was doing the pouring of the peas (Note 28, above), though the justification for this is by no means clear. Schofield (1913) (pp. 145 & 146) has argued very persuasively that "peas" is, in any case, a mistranslation of the mediæval French word "pois" or "poys," meaning "pitch".

Chaucer's *The Legend of Cleopatra*

The Battle of Actium, 2 September 31 BC
Lorenzo A. Castro (Laureys a Castro), 1672
© *National Maritime Museum, Greenwich, London*

The havoc wreaked upon Antony's fleet is vividly depicted in this painting, though the boat in which Cleopatra is shown escaping would have been far too small to undertake the long sea voyage to Egypt that was contemplated: it is, moreover, powered only by two pairs of oars and its only sail (at the prow) appears to show the wind blowing against the boat's intended direction of travel. If Cleopatra had, as has been suggested, pre-planned her escape from Actium should the battle go against Antony's fleet, her ship would have been equipped with large sails suitable for a long but speedy sea crossing, rather than with the smaller sails which would be needed to make the rapid manoeuvres required in battle. There is no sign on Cleopatra's vessel, as it is shown in this painting, of the purple sails referred to by Lucius Annæus Florus, Vincent de Beauvais, Giovanni Boccaccio and Chaucer (pp. 85 & 86, Chapter 9 and the Appendices; see also the illustration on p. 62).

30. ... the queen, with her purple sails

The only reference to "purple sails" in the Roman literature is to be found in Plutarch's account of the life of Antony. When Cleopatra was summoned to present herself to Antony in Tarsus, she sailed in her golden barge up the River Cydnus to that city, and Plutarch's description of how the purple sails had "billowed in the wind," was taken, along with a number of other details, by Shakespeare when he described in *Antony and Cleopatra* how:

> The barge she sat in, like a burnish'd throne,
> Burned on the water: the poop was beaten gold;
> Purple the sails, and so perfumèd that
> The winds were love-sick with them ...
>
> *William Shakespeare (1600–1612)*

This apparent conflation of the story of the golden barge and the account of the Battle of Actium occurs in the second-century AD *Epitome Rerum Romanorum* of Lucius Annæus Florus, and again, around 1220 AD, in the *Speculum Historiale* (*The Mirror of History*) of Vincent de Beauvais, though this latter account seems to have been taken directly from Florus. The mention of the purple sails is the primary reason for some writers having proposed that the writings of Florus and/or Vincent were Chaucer's principal sources for *The Legend of*

Cleopatra (see also Chapter 9, and Appendices I and II). The illustration on p. 62 shows how this notion of the purple sails persisted even into the twentieth century.

31. ... that chance being taken

    The word "aventure," is the Old English derivative of the Old French "auenture" (Latin: "adventura"), meaning "a thing about to happen." Jones (1971) has suggested that, in the present context, it could be read figuratively as "saw that state of affairs," though better might be "saw that happen" or "saw that opportunity (or chance) being taken."

32. Before he went out of the place of battle

    The accounts of Florus and Vincent de Beauvais (Appendices I & II) are so short that the relative timing of events is not always clear, and they have sometimes been read as asserting that Antony killed himself in 31 BC immediately after the Battle of Actium. Though this would support the view that these accounts were Chaucer's primary sources, both could also be interpreted as placing Antony's suicide in 30 BC in Egypt.

33. And had the body embalmed ...

    It must surely have been clear to Chaucer that by having Antony commit suicide on seeing Cleopatra make her escape from the Battle of Actium, he was creating an incompatibility with the remainder of the poem, which fails to explain how Antony's body was recovered by Cleopatra and then taken by her to Egypt to be embalmed and interred, unless it is assumed that the ship which bore Antony's body followed that of Cleopatra to Egypt.

34. And beside the shrine she then dug a pit
This is probably a misreading of the Latin sources which said that Cleopatra wished to be buried not beside the *shrine* but beside *Antony*.

35. ... all the snakes that she could obtain
Plutarch referred to a single asp, and Shakespeare and Boccaccio to two. Only Florus and Vincent de Beauvais wrote about a greater plurality of snakes (pp. 150 & 151, and the Appendices).

36. ... and spoke thus
The length of this speech reflects that presented in Plutarch. The equivalent speech is similarly lengthy in Shakespeare's *Antony and Cleopatra*.

37. In happiness or in sorrow, in song or in dance
Lynch (1972) suggests that this links two proverbial phrases. "For wele or wo" may also be a rephrasing of the marriage vow "For better or for worse."

38. Inasmuch as it lay in my power
An alternative phrasing would be "As far as I was able to do so." "Inasmuch" could also be rendered "Insofar."

39.. ... naked, and with an unwavering heart
Skeat (1889) believes that Chaucer mistranslated the Latin "induta," meaning "clothed" or "a putting on (of clothes)," when he referred to Cleopatra as being naked (the suggestion is presumably that he misread the word as "nuda"). Although Cleopatra is depicted in a state of nudity or semi-nudity by the majority of the artists who have represented her in paintings, all the accounts given by the ancient historians emphasize that she committed suicide whilst dressed in her royal garments.

40. I pray to God that our heads shall not ache!
The ending of this poem on what seems a casual or even flippant note has given rise to much discussion (see p. 164). Contentious, too, is "Amen" added after the last line (the only *Legend* in which this occurs). *The Legend of Good Women* was written to be read to an audience, and Quinn (1994) has argued that Chaucer intended his listeners to have an amused response to it: could it be that Chaucer would deliver "Amen" as "Ah! *Men!*"?

5

Glossary

agayn: again
ake: ache
al, alle: all
algates: always, in any case, at all costs, in every way
al-outerly, al-uterly: utterly, completely, solely, entirely
anoon, anon: anon, soon
armes: weapons, armour, battle
at-ones, atones: at once, together
aventure: a thing about to happen, state of affairs.
ay: ever, again
been, ben: be
beginneth, begynneth: begins, starts
behynd: behind
bereth: bears, carries
beste: best
biddeth: bids, tells
blisful: blissful
blythe: blithe, happy, pleased, cheerful, in good spirits
bokes: books, history books
bounden: bound, tied up, ensnared
breeth, breth: breath

bringeth: brings
broght: brought, led
buryinge: burial
but-if: unless
byhynd: behind
carole: carol, singing, a round dance with singing
cas: case, event, happening
certeinly, certeynly: certainly, in fact
Cesar: Caesar; Octavian
charge: load, significance, importance
cheere, chere: cheer
chees, ches: choose, chose
chivalrye: chivalry, knighthood
conqueren: conquer, win, gain
cors: body
coude: could
covenant, covenaunt: vow, pledge, contract, agreement
crewel: cruel
crokes: crooks, (sharp) hooks
cuppe: cup, goblet
damage: loss, misfortune, sadness (Fr. *domage*)
daunce: dance, dancing
dede: dead
deeth, deth; death
dere: dear, precious
desert: merit, virtue, quality

Glossary

destresse, distresse: distress, trouble
destruccioun: destruction
devyse: describe, relate, talk about
deye, dye: die
discrecioun: thoughtfulness, wisdom, moral awareness
dispayre: dispair, loss of hope
doun: down
dryveth: drives, pushes
due: necessary, needful, rightful, just, obligatory
dwelle: delay
eek, ek: also, as well, moreover
effect: importance, meaning, substance
Egipt, Egipte: Egypt
embaume: embalm
emprise, empryse: undertaking, enterprise, venture
ende: an end
er: before, until
espie, espye: see, look for, find
faile, fayle: avoid, doubt, be unsuccessful
falsly: falsely
fayr: fair
fele, felen: feel, experience
felten: felt, experienced
ferforth: much, inasmuch, insofar, as far as
ferforthly: greatly, completely
ferther: further, far

feste: feast, festivities, ceremony, banquet
fette: fetched, brought
fyght: fighting
fil: fell, befell, happened
fle, flee: flee, run away, escape
fleeth, fleth: flees, runs away, escapes
flighte, flyghte: flight
folk: men
for-sooth, for-sothe: in truth, truly
forthy: therefore, consequently
frely: freely, unreservedly, willingly
fro: from
ful: very, full
fulfille: fulfil
fynde: find
fyne: fine
gentil: worthy, excellent, noble, gracious, kind
gentilesse, gentillese: worthiness, excellence
gonne: gun
goon, gon: go
goth: goes (*as in* "there goes the …")
governyng: governance, rule, control
grapenel: grappling-hook
grave: dig, carve
greet, gret, grete: great, big, large, important
grisly, grisely: dreadful, unpleasant, grim, frightening

Glossary

hacches, haches: hatches
hadde: had
han: have
happed, happede: happened, occurred, came about
hardinesse, hardynesse: strength, boldness, daring
hayl: hail
hedes: heads, brains
heer: here
hem: them
her, hir, hire, hyre: her, to her
herkneth: listen, hear, attend, pay attention
herte: heart
heterly: fiercely, violently
him, hym: him, to him
hit: it
hokes: hooks
houre: hour, time
hurtelen, hurtlen: attack, knock, dash
hymself: himself
in: in, to
knyght: knight
kyndenesse: kindness, affection, love, devotion
kyng: king
lafte: left, deserted, departed
las: snare, trap
laste: end

lasteth: lasts, remains, keeps going

lat: let, permit, allow (see also *leet, lete,* below)

lede: lead, conduct, bring

leet, lete: let, allowed (see also *lat,* above)

lenger, lengere: longer

leoun, lyoun: lions

leste: desire, pleasure, delight, wish, whim, lust

liven: living, alive

longe: long

lorn: lost

lovede: loved

lye: lie, deceive

lyf: life

lyke: like, similar to

lym, lyme: lime, quick-lime

maad: made, produced, written

maken: make, produce, create, write

mene: mean, refer to, signify

mete, meten: meet, encounter, engage

mighte, myghte: might, could, be able to, have power to

morwe: morning, morrow, next day

myn: my

narwe: narrowly, tightly, closely

nas: is not

nat: not

ne: not

Glossary

nedderes, neddres: adders
nere: never, not
nevere: never
nis: is not
noon, non: no, none
nyght: night
obeisaunce, obeÿsaunce: obedience, control, submission
obeyede: obeyed
Octovian, Octovyan: Octavian
oghte, oughte: ought, owed
oth: oath
or (er): before, until
ord, orde: point, tip
ost: host
oure: our
overbord, over-borde: overboard
persone: person, personality, individual
pesen: peas
peynen: took care, took pains
polax: poleaxe, battle-axe
pottes: pots, jars
poureth: pours, poured
pray, preye: pray, beseech, beg, ask, request
presseth: press, thrust forward, strive towards
prosperite, prosperitee: prosperity, good fortune, success
purpe: purple, purple cloth

putte: put, placed, filled
queene, quene: queen
quod: quoth, said
receyveth: receives, received
reed, red: advice, counsel, guidance, plan
regned: reigned, ruled
regnes: realms, kingdoms
remembraunce: remembrance, memory
remenaunt: remainder, the rest
renne: run, hasten, hurry, come quickly
right, ryght: right, justice, just treatment, just claim
right/ryght swiche: whatever
rof, roof: stabbed, lacerated
roghte, roughte: cared
Romains, Romeyns: Romans
routhe: lamenting, pity, wailing, compassion, mercy
rubyes: rubies
saile, sayl, sayle: sail
schent, shent: destroyed, defeated, disgraced, shamed
se, see: sea
seen, sen: see
sene: seen, visible, evident, manifest
senatour: senator
sette: set (the gaze), perceive, observe
seyde: said
seye, seyne: say, tell, speak

Glossary

seyl: sail

shame: shame, disgrace

serpents, serpentes: snakes

shering-hokes, sherynge-hokes: shearing-hooks

shete: shoot, shooting

shette: shut, enclosed, locked, fastened

sholde, shulde: should

shoop, shop: created, built up, assembled, raised

shortly: briefly, in brief, shortly, concisely

shoute: shout, shouting

shippe: ship

shryne: shrine, mausoleum, tomb

sithe, sythe: scythe

skippe, skyppe: skip, miss out, omit, jump, go quickly (to)

slake: diminish, reduce, decrease

slider, slidere: (make) slippery

slippe: slip, pass, pass over

sonne: sun

sooth, soth: truth, true thing

sorweful: sorrowful, sad, grieving

soun: sound, noise

speke, speken: speak, talk of, utter

spende: spend, expend

speres: spear's

spycerye: spice, spices

stente: wait, stop, cease, leave off, refrain

stable: constant (in affection), faithful, steadfast
sterte: start, make a quick movement
sterve: die
stinge, stynge: sting, bite
stingeth, styngeth: pierces, cuts, stabs
storial, storyal: historical
stoute: stout, strong
strokes: things thrown, missile
stryf: strife, disagreement, enmity
subtil: skilled, clever, ingenious
suster: sister
sweren: swear (an oath), affirm, assent, pledge
swich, swiche: such
swor: swore, vowed, pledged
telle: tell, recount, relate
than, thanne: then
theffect, th'effect: the important things/matters
ther: there, then
thikke: thick, thickly
thilke: that very (same)
thynge: thing
thise: these
tho: then
thoughte: thought, had an idea
thourgh: because of
thourghout: through, throughout

Glossary

til, tyl: until
to: to, too
to-gider, togidere: together
to-go: scatter, run away, escape
took, tok: took
toun: town
trewe: true, genuine, proper, faithful, honest
trewer: truer, more faithful
trompe: trumpet
trouthe: truth, truthfulness, fidelity, loyalty, constancy
tyl: until
tyme: time
unreprovable: irreproachable, beyond reproof
usaunce: custom, habit
wakynge: waking, awake, vigilant
war: aware, knew, informed, realized (it)
weddynge: wedding
wel, wele: prosperity, happiness, good fortune, success
wente: went
werreyour: warrior, soldier
wemen, women: a woman
werkmen: workmen, craftsmen
wex: became, grew into
whan: when, after, since
what that: when, as soon as
whiche: which

whil, whyl: whilst

wif, wyf: wife

wight, wyght: creature, being, person, man

wit, witte: mind, wits, senses, reason

wo: adversity, sadness, sorrow, misfortune

wod, wood: mad, maddened, angry, furious, enraged

woful: woeful, sad, sorrowful, unfortunate

wol: will

wolde: wish, want

worshipe: honour, respect, dignity, reputation

worthi, worthy: worthy, noble, deserving, honourable

wroth: angry, angered

wyfhood: wifehood, wifely duty

youre: your

yow: you

ytake, y-take: undertaken, engaged in

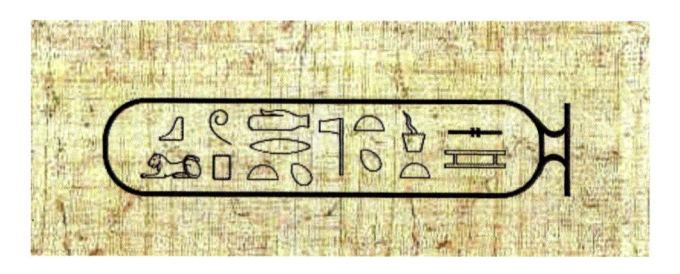

Cartouche (name ring) of Cleopatra

Egyptian hieroglyphic form of the praenomen (first name) and nomen (throne name) of Cleopatra. This reads: "The goddess Cleopatra, who is beloved of her father." The Greek form of the name Cleopatra (Κλεοπατρα) is derived from κλεος *(kleos:* glory) and πατρος *(patros:* of the father). © *Marius Press.*

6

Three Modern English Versions of *The Legend of Cleopatra*

The form of the three versions

Three distinct Modern English versions of *The Legend of Cleopatra* are now presented.

The first of these is a plain-text version, taken mainly from the reorganised and rephrased Modern English lines given in Chapter 4, with some adjustments to make the text flow more easily. Pairs of lines are presented as non-rhyming couplets of varying numbers of syllables and of different meters (see below). This forms the basis upon which the subsequent two new rhyming metric versions have been based.

Modern English Rhyming version 1 is constructed as a series of couplets, written as iambic tetrameters; whilst in the Modern English Rhyming version 2, the couplets are composed of iambic pentameters (see below).

Prosodic terms

An *iamb* (or an *iambic foot*, as it is sometimes termed) is a two-syllable unit, the first syllable of which is unstressed (o) and the second **stressed** (●).

Thus the line:

> Her death she then received, with full good cheer

would be read as:

/ Her **death** / she **then** / re **ceived**, / with **full** / good **cheer** /
/ o • / o • / o • / o • / o • /

This has *five* iambic feet (/o•/), and the meter (rhythm) is thus referred to as a *penta*meter. A line with only *four* iambic feet is a *tetra*meter. For example:

/ Her **end** / she **met** / with **full** / good **cheer** /
/ o • / o • / o • / o • /

Whilst both the modern-language rhyming versions clearly take some liberties with the Chaucerian wording, the primary purpose of each is to keep the "feel" of the poem as close as possible to that of the original.

Though the version written in iambic tetrameters is certainly much jauntier than that written in iambic pentameters, and may thereby better reflect the mood of Chaucer's original poem, it is nevertheless the latter – the iambic pentameter version – that is closest to Chaucer's poem in both form and style. It is important to remember, though, that Chaucer was not at all obsessional about keeping to an iambic pentameter rhythm, and did not hesitate either to drop a syllable or to add one if his artistic purposes were best served by doing so.

Three Modern English Versions

Modern English non-rhyming version

After the death of Ptolemy, the king
    Who ruled over the whole of Egypt,
His queen, Cleopatra, reigned
    Until there came a time when it happened
That a senator was sent from Rome
    To conquer kingdoms, and win honour
For Rome, for it was its custom
    To bring the world under its rule;
And, in truth, his name was Antony.
    And, as Fortune owed him a disgrace
(Because he had been successful),
    He was repudiated by Rome;
And, moreover, Caesar's sister
    Had been deserted by him, before she realized,
For he wished always to take another as his wife.
    He thus quarrelled with both Rome and Caesar.
Nevertheless, this same senator was, in truth,
    A very worthy, noble soldier,
And his death was met with great sadness.
    Love, however, had made him so foolhardy,
And bound him so tightly in its snare
    All for the love of Cleopatra

Chaucer's *The Legend of Cleopatra*

That he valued nothing in all the world,
    And thought nothing so important to him
As loving and serving Cleopatra.
    He did not care if he died in battle
If it were in defence of her and of her right.
    The noble queen dearly loved this knight,
For all his qualities and for his chivalry;
    And certainly, if the history books do not lie,
He was, in personality and nobility
    And in soundness of judgement and strength,
As worthy as any living man.
    And she was as fair as the rose in May.
And – for it is best to keep the story short –
    She became his wife, and had him as she desired.
To describe the wedding and the feast,
    Would, for me, who has undertaken the task
Of recounting so many stories,
    Take too long, and I might make too little of
Things of more importance and significance;
    (For men may overload a ship or barge!).
Therefore I will skip to important matters,
    And I will drop the rest.
Octavian, who was enraged by this deed,
    Raised an army to lead against Antony,
Solely for his destruction,
    With stout Romans, cruel as lions;

Three Modern English Versions

They went to their ships and set sail. I leave them thus.
    Antony, aware of this, wished not to fail
To engage with the Roman fleet, if he could.
    He therefore made his plans, and then one day both
His wife and he, with all his men, went
    To board their ships, waiting no longer.
At sea they met in battle –
    The battle-horn called, men shouted, missiles flew.
Antony's men took care to keep their backs to the sun.
    With a terrible sound a huge catapult fired,
And the fleets fiercely attacked each other.
    From above fell great rocks.
In went the grappling-hooks, bristling with claws,
    Among the ropes, and in ran the shear-hooks, too.
Men with battle-axes fought each other;
    One man ran behind the mast,
And then out again, driving another overboard;
    One man stabbed himself with his spear;
Another slashed the sail with scythe-like hooks;
    Another, bearing a goblet, bade everyone be cheerful!
One poured peas on the hatches, to make them slippery.
    With pots of quicklime, men rushed at each other.
And thus they spent the long day fighting,
    Until, at last, as all things must come to an end,
Antony was defeated, and put to flight,
    His men escaping as best they could.

The queen fled too, with her purple sails,
    From the missiles which fell as thick as hail –
It was no wonder she could not endure it.
    When Antony saw that happen,
"Alas," he said, "I rue the day that I was born!
    This day I have lost all honour!"
And, driven out of his mind by despair,
    He at once stabbed himself through his heart
Before he had left the battle scene.
    His wife, who could expect no mercy from Caesar,
Fled to Egypt, fearful and distressed.
    But listen, all you who speak of love,
You men, who falsely swear many an oath,
    That you would die were your loved one angered,
Here may you see such truth in a woman!
    The disconsolate Cleopatra grieved so much
That there is no language to describe it.
    However, the next day, not wishing to delay,
She bade her skilled workmen build a shrine,
    Using all the rubies and fine gemstones
That she could find in the whole of Egypt.
    And she filled the shrine with spices.
And the body she had embalmed, and she fetched
    This dead body and locked it in the shrine.
And next to the shrine she dug a pit;
    And all the snakes that she could obtain

Three Modern English Versions

She put into the pit, saying:
    "Now, my beloved, whom my sad heart obeyed
So completely that, from that happy time
    When I swore that I would willingly be yours
(I mean you, Antony, my knight!),
    Never while I remained awake, day or night,
Were you ever out of my memory in my heart,
    Whether I was happy or sad, singing or dancing.
And I then made this pledge to myself, that
    Whatever you were to feel – happiness or sorrow –
Inasmuch as it lay in my power,
    And ever faithful to my wifely duty,
I would feel the same – in life or death.
    And, whilst I still breathe, that very pledge
I shall fulfil – and that shall be clearly seen.
    Never was a queen truer to her loved one."
And thus saying, naked, and with cheerful heart,
    She threw herself into the pit, among the snakes.
And there she chose to be buried.
    The snakes immediately began to sting her,
And she accepted her death cheerfully,
    For the love of Antony, who was so dear to her.
And all this is historical fact: it is not a fable!
    Now, until I find a man as true and faithful as this,
And who would so willingly die for his love,
    I pray to God that our heads shall never ache!

Chaucer's *The Legend of Cleopatra*

Antony and Cleopatra Dissolving the Pearl in Wine
Andrea Casali, date unknown (between 1725 and 1784)
Hinton Ampner Collection. © National Trust Images

The incident in which Cleopatra is said to have dissolved a pearl in wine, although described by Boccaccio (see Appendix III), is not mentioned by Chaucer. With regard to Cleopatra's dress, it was common for her to be depicted wearing clothes of a much later era than those she would have worn at the time of her liaison with Antony. The Roman men who were depicted were, however, almost always shown in their traditional Roman military attire. Can one perhaps conclude from this that whilst the men in Cleopatra's life were of their time, she herself – or at least the character that was assigned to her in literature and art – was regarded as timeless? See also: *Cleopatra and the Dying Mark Antony* by Batoni (p. 40); *Cleopatra on the Terraces of Philae* by Bridgman (p. 54); *The Meeting of Antony and Cleopatra* by Tiepolo (p. 73); *The Deaths of Antony and Cleopatra* (p. 138); *Cleopatra Delivering her Life to the Serpents* (p. 157); and *Cleopatra and Octavian* by Gauffier (p. 166).

Three Modern English Versions

Modern English rhyming version 1 (tetrameters)

When came the death of Ptolemy
    (All Egypt for his realm had he),
'Twas then Queen Cleopatra reigned
    Till came a day it was ordained
That out of Rome a senator
    Should come to conquer kings – the more
To honour Rome. Thus should it be,
    For Rome would hold the world in fee.
The senator was Antony.
    A victim to base Fortune, he.
Though Chance and Fate had served him well
    'Gainst Rome did Antony rebel.
The sister of Octavian,
    He falsely left. It was his plan
To take another as his wife,
    And this in Rome had caused great strife.
And yet, in truth, this senator,
    A noble, worthy warrior,
Was mourned when he untimely died.
    His sanity by love was tried,
And madness caught him in its snare.
    He loved so much, he did not care

To value what the world might give.
    His need was only this – to live
And to his wife his love to bring:
    To die in war a minor thing,
Defending Cleopatra's right!
    The queen, she loved this noble Knight,
His merits and his chivalry.
    And – if we trust to history –
Nobility was in him, too;
    And wisdom, strength, and derring-do.
No greater man lived in that day!
    And she? Fair as the rose in May!
To keep it short (for short is life!)
    She wed him, and became his wife.
"What of the wedding?" you may ask;
    So burdened am I by the task
Of telling tale … then tale … then tale,
    That, in long-telling, might I fail
To speak of things I should enlarge
    (As men may overload a barge!)
So, to important things I skip.
    The rest of it – I let it slip!
Octavian, by fury crazed,
    A great and fearsome army raised;
For Antony he would lay waste.
    The cruel Romans thus made haste

Three Modern English Versions

To board their ships, and then set sail.
    Said Antony, "I shall not fail
To meet this Roman fleet at sea."
    His plans complete, his wife and he,
And all his men, went forth one day –
    The battle they would not delay.
At sea, the ships converged – and then
    The horn was heard! And shouts of men!
And Antony, the sun to rear,
    The mighty missile's surge could hear.
And man on man then fiercely fought.
    Great stones rained down and ruin brought.
In went the grapnels' grasping nails,
    Whilst shear-hooks seized the billowed sails.
Huge axes swung from side to side;
    Behind the mast a man would hide,
Then overboard his foe would fling
    (Else, with his spear himself would sting!).
With scythe-like hooks, the sails were rent.
    Some, quaffing wine, called "Be content!"
Then made with peas the hatches slick!
    Or clashed with pots of quick-lime thick.
The battle raged throughout the day,
    Then ended (all things do, they say)
When Antony was put to flight;
    His forces fled, as best they might.

Chaucer's *The Legend of Cleopatra*

As did his queen, 'neath purple sail,
    Escape the missiles, thick as hail.
(Too dreadful was it to sustain.)
    But this, to Antony, was pain.
He rued the moment of his birth:
    "Respect for me has now no worth!"
A madness grew from his despair:
    He stabbed his heart through, then and there,
Before he left the battled sea.
    No mercy for his wife would be,
So she to Egypt fled, distraught.
    Now listen closely – as you ought –
You men, who falsely swear an oath
    To die for her that holds your troth,
Regard this woman – faithful, she!
    How Cleopatra wept! (There be
No tongue her suffering can say.)
    The morrow, brooked she no delay,
But bade her craftsmen build a shrine
    Of all the rubies, gemstones fine,
That Egypt held. 'Twas as she willed.
    The shrine she then with spices filled;
Embalmed, beloved Antony
    Was locked into the shrine, and she
Had by the shrine a deep pit mined,
    And all the snakes that she might find

Three Modern English Versions

Were put into its earthen shade.
    "Belovèd, whom my heart obeyed,
Without default," she freely wept,
    "Oh, I was yours. This pledge I kept.
For you, oh Antony, my knight,
    In day or in the darkling night,
Were ever in my heart's recall,
    Though health or illness might befall.
And to myself this vow I spelt,
    That, well or ill – what e're you felt –
As much as in my pow'r it lay,
    I would, as faithful wife, thus pray
To feel the same – in life or death –
    And that this vow, whilst I have breath,
I should fulfil, that all might say
    'No truer queen saw light of day!' "
Then Cleopatra, pledge full kept,
    Among the serpents, naked, leaped
To death upon herself to bring,
    As came it did, with poisoned sting.
Her end she met – and with good cheer
    For love of Antony, so dear.
No fable have I told to you.
    And ere I find a man as true
Who will for love his own life take
    I pray our heads shall never ache!

Chaucer's *The Legend of Cleopatra*

Modern English rhyming version 2 (pentameters)

When came the death of Ptolemy, the king
    Who held all Egypt in his governing,
His queen, named Cleopatra, then she reigned
    Until there came a day it was ordained
That out of Rome was sent a senator
    To conquer kingdoms and reap honour for
The town of Rome which, as was custom then,
    Would dominate and rule the world of men;
And Antony (I tell the truth) his name.
    Now, Fortune, at that time, owed him a shame:
Prosperity was his, but – so they tell –
    He did against the town of Rome rebel.
His Roman wife (and Caesar's sister, she!),
    He falsely left, before she knew that he
Had set his heart upon another wife –
    And this, with Rome and Caesar, caused great strife.
Despite it all, in truth, this senator
    Was worthy, and a noble warrior;
His dying brought great sadness, it was said,
    But Love to madness had this poor man led,
And then had tightly bound him in its snare.
    Held, for the love of Cleopatra, there,

Three Modern English Versions

He valued nothing that the world might hold,
    Save one thing only, as it has been told –
To love his Cleopatra, whom he'd serve;
    Nor yet from death in battle would he swerve
In his defence of her, and of her right.
    The noble queen, she likewise loved the knight,
For all his merits and his chivalry;
    And it is true (if truth in books there be!)
He was of noble personality;
    As wise and hardy as a man may be;
Full worthy, too, as any of that day.
    And she was fair as is the rose in May.
To keep my story short (for short is life!)
    She took her knight, and thus became his wife.
The wedding and the feast I'll not recount:
    I fear the task too great would it amount –
So many stories do I have to tell
    I might omit (as I do know full well)
Those things on which 'twere best I should enlarge
    (For men may overload a ship or barge!)
And therefore to important things I skip,
    As for the rest – well, I shall let it slip.
Octavian by fury was so crazed
    That he a great and fearsome army raised –
For Antony, he vowed, he would lay waste –
    Then bade his cruel Romans to make haste

To board upon their ships, and then set sail.
    Said Antony, aware, "I shall not fail
To meet this Roman fleet upon the sea."
    When all his plans were made, his wife and he
With all his fighting men went forth one day
    And put to sea, no longer to delay;
There met the fleets. The horn was blown! And then
    Came sounds of missiles, and the shouts of men.
T'was best to keep the sun behind, they found.
    The catapults flung rocks, with dreadful sound.
And, fiercely, ship 'gainst fighting ship would fly;
    Down fell the crushing rocks, as from the sky.
In went the grappling-hooks with grasping claws,
    The shear-hooks seizing canvas in their jaws.
The battle-axes swung from side to side;
    Behind a mast a man would run to hide,
Then out again, another to un-ship –
    Or spike himself upon his spear's sharp tip!
The sails were rent with hooks, as with a scythe.
    A man who raised his cup bade all be blithe!
Poured peas made all the hatches slick as slime;
    And men would rush at men with pots of lime.
Thus did the fighting rage throughout the day,
    And then it ended – all things do, they say!
And Antony, defeated, took to flight;
    His forces then escaped as best they might.

Three Modern English Versions

Fled, too, the queen, beneath her purple sail,
    From missiles striking down, as thick as hail.
(It is no wonder she could not remain.)
    But her escape gave Antony great pain.
"I rue," said he, "the day that I was born!
    All hope for my respect is now forlorn."
And from such bleak despair did madness start:
    He then took up his sword and pierced his heart
Before he left that battle on the sea.
    No mercy then would Cleopatra see,
And thus to Egypt fled, in fear, distressed.
    Now you who think yourselves of honour blest,
You men, who swear so readily an oath
    That you will die for her who holds your troth,
See here a woman of fidelity.
    For Cleopatra so lament did she
There is no tongue that has the words to say.
    But on the morrow brooked she no delay,
Commanding her skilled workmen craft a shrine
    Of all the rubies and the gemstones fine
That she, in all of Egypt, could espy;
    And filled the shrine with spices, by and by.
The body, when embalmed, was then conveyed
    Unto the shrine, and there was sadly laid.
Beside the shrine a pit she then had mined;
    And all the poison-snakes that she might find,

Chaucer's *The Legend of Cleopatra*

She put them in that grave, and said at last:
    "My love, to whom my saddened heart held fast,
As so it has, e'er since that hour of bliss
    I swore I would be yours to love and kiss,
I say to you, oh Antony, my knight,
    That in my waking hours, both day and night,
You were for ever in my heart's recall
    In song or dance, though good or ill befall.
And to myself this solemn pledge I spelt,
    That, well or ill – as ever that you felt –
As far as in my power that it lay,
    Thus faithful to my wifehood, I would pray
To feel the same – and this in life or death!
    That covenant, while in me lasts a breath,
I shall fulfil, and it shall well be seen –
    Was never to her love a truer queen!"
Thus saying, naked, then her pledge she kept –
    Among the serpents in the pit she leaped.
'Twas there she chose to have her burying,
    And there, anon, she felt the serpents' sting.
Her death she then received, with full good cheer,
    For love of Antony, to her so dear.
I swear no fable have I told to you!
    Until I find a man who is thus true,
And will, for love, his death so freely take,
    I pray to God our heads shall never ache!

7

Queen Anne and
The Legend of Good Women

It was been proposed by a number of scholars that not only did Chaucer undertake the writing of *The Legend of Good Women* at the command of Queen Anne, the queen consort of Richard II, but that, in discharging this task, he had been constrained by the Queen's rigid prescription of the form that the poem should take and of the tenor of the message it should convey.

What, though, is the evidence for this? Before looking for any clues which may exist within the poem itself, let us take a brief overview of the life of Queen Anne, to see how this overlapped, and was to some extent interlinked with, that of Chaucer.

The life of Queen Anne

Anne of Bohemia was born on 11 May 1366 into the House of Luxemburg, the eldest daughter of Elizabeth of Pomerania and Charles IV, King of Bohemia and Holy Roman Emperor.

She had received a sound education (her father had founded the University of Prague), and was said to have possessed a gentle disposition. She was also, according to several reports, outstandingly beautiful – though Brewer (1978) says that she was "plain but kind."

When she was 15 years old, a marriage was arranged between her and King Richard II of England. She arrived in England in December 1381, and shortly afterwards, on 22 January 1382, the wedding took place in London and she was crowned Queen consort. Richard, like Anne, was only 15 at the time.

The marriage met with resistance amongst the English politicians and various members of the nobility, primarily because there was no great political or – what was just as important – financial advantage to be gained from it. In fact, not only did Anne come to the marriage without a dowry, but Richard actually paid 20,000 florins to her family (specifically, to her brother Wenceslas).

At a personal level, the marriage was an unqualified success, the young couple being deeply devoted to each other. Anne and her courtiers were, however, regarded as profligate: she was highly fashion-conscious, promoting, for example, the wearing by women of pointed shoes and padded shoulders, as well as the two-foot-tall horned and gauze-draped head-dress. She may have been responsible, too, for introducing into England the decorous side-saddle mode of horse riding for women. Moreover, the fondness which she and Richard showed for dancing and

Queen Anne and *The Legend of Good Women*

Anne of Bohemia, Queen Consort to Richard II
English School (18th century): Coloured engraving, printed by
Henry G. Bohn, 1856

© *Bridgeman Images/Private Collection/Prismatic Pictures*

throwing lavish parties was generally frowned upon, though perhaps unreasonably – the royal couple were, after all, still very young.

Despite this, it soon became apparent that Anne was gracious, compassionate, and able to influence Richard in the decisions he made affecting both individuals and the community. These qualities had been demonstrated even before she came to England to be married, when she had interceded with Richard on behalf of some of those who had participated in the Peasants' Revolt of 1381, securing pardons for all of them. She was later successful in a number of other important cases, including, in 1384, persuading Richard (she threw herself upon her knees before him) to commute the death sentence imposed upon ex-mayor of London, John Northampton, who had been indicted for provoking insurrection – though a similarly theatrical intercession before the 1388 so-called Merciless Parliament on behalf of Sir Simon de Burley failed. She was prominent in protecting the religious reformer John Wycliffe from prosecution, probably saving his life.

Most importantly, Anne's calming influence lay behind Richard's reversal of his decision to transfer the royal courts from London to York, which had led to the capital city's experiencing a drop not only in its prestige but also in the substantial commercial income which the presence of the courts greatly encouraged. After parading through the streets of London to celebrate the King's reconciliation with the city the royal couple went to Westminster Hall, where Anne is said to have prostrated herself before her husband, begging him to go even further and restore all the city's ancient rights – a request which Richard duly granted.

Through these and other acts Anne, by proving to be a moderating influence on Richard, became widely admired and acclaimed for her humanity. Her intercessions on behalf of the common folk greatly endeared her to the general public and resulted in the appellation of "Good Queen Anne." This aspect of her reputation was further enhanced by her benevolent concern for the welfare of women, and pregnant women in particular – a concern which probably had its roots in her own inability to produce an heir for Richard. When Anne died, on 7 June 1394, aged 28, she had, to Richard's lasting despair, remained childless after twelve years of marriage.

Anne's death, most likely of the plague, occurred at Sheen Manor, a large house on the edge of the River Thames, upstream from Westminster Palace. The manor house had been substantially renovated by Edward III shortly before his death, and was taken over by Richard II as his primary residence one year after his marriage to Anne of Bohemia. It was there that he and his young queen had spent some of their happiest times together.

Richard, in an excess of grief at the death of his beloved Anne, ordered the house to be destroyed. It was not until 20 years later that the ruins were cleared and the house, now named Richmond Palace, was rebuilt by Henry V.

Chronology

The sequence in which several of Chaucer's major works were written is shown below (the dates are necessarily approximate) in the context of various events in his life, as well as in the lives of some of the royal personages with whom he was acquainted.

1340?	Chaucer born
1366	Anne of Bohemia born
Pre-1368	*Romaunt of the Rose* (part translation)
1368	Chaucer valet, then Esquire, to Edward III; death of Blanche, wife of John of Gaunt
1368–1369	*The Book of the Duchess*
1369–1378	Chaucer makes various trips abroad
1374	Chaucer becomes Customs Comptroller (Wool, Skin and Hides)
1377	Death of Edward III; accession of Richard II
1377–1379	*The House of Fame*
1381	The Peasants' Revolt
1382	*The Parlement of Foules*; Chaucer becomes Customs Comptroller (Wine); marriage of Richard II and Anne of Bohemia; coronation of Anne
1382–1385	*Troilus and Criseyde*
1385	Chaucer becomes Justice of the Peace (Kent) and Member of Parliament (Kent)

Queen Anne and *The Legend of Good Women*

1385/6–?	*The Legend of Good Women*
1386–?	*The Canterbury Tales*
1389	Chaucer, no longer a Member of Parliament or Justice of the Peace, becomes Clerk of the King's Works
1391	Chaucer resigns as Clerk of the King's works, becoming Deputy Forester for the Forest of North Pemberton
1394	Queen Anne dies
1399	Richard II overthrown by Henry Bolingbroke (Henry IV); death of John of Gaunt
1400	Richard II murdered in prison; Chaucer dies.

Chaucer, a well-known public figure, would have been a frequent visitor to the royal court, and it is certain that he and Anne would have been well acquainted with each other. As we can see, his work *Troilus and Criseyde* was written when Anne, now eighteen years old, had been on the throne for three years.

Evidence for the influence of Queen Anne

At the time that Chaucer's *Troilus and Criseyde* appeared, the devotion which Anne and her husband had for each other would have been apparent to all, and Anne's firmly held views on the importance of chastity, moral virtue, constancy and faithfulness in love widely recognised. Moreover, Anne's reputation for interceding with Richard, and thus the public view of her as a "good woman," would already have been well established.

Chaucer's *The Legend of Cleopatra*

Could it be that Anne was concerned that in *Troilus and Criseyde* Chaucer had dwelt upon the fickleness of women – exemplified by Criseyde (Cressida), who had taken Troilus as her lover, only to dismiss him and turn instead to Diomede (Diomedes)? And had Anne already been disturbed by Chaucer's translation of the *Roman de la Rose*, perhaps feeling that he had, in a sense, been complicit with its two French authors in promulgating a view of all women as unchaste and unfaithful?

It was John Lydgate of Bury (ca.1370 – ca.1451), a monk, poet, and avowed admirer of Chaucer's work, who asserted most clearly that Chaucer had been commanded by Queen Anne to write *The Legend of Good Women* as a form of penance for his previous negative treatments of women. Advancing this view in his *The Fall of Princes* (ca. 1431–1439), Lydgate remarked that whilst Chaucer had intended to write about 19 "good women," he could not, when it came down to it, call quite so many to mind!

> This poete wrote at Request of the quene
> A Legende of parfight hoolynesse
> Off goode womon to Fynden out nyntene
> That did excelle in bounte and fayrnesse,
> But for his labour and his besynesse
> Was importable his wittes to encoumbre
> In al the world to Fynde so greet a noumbre …
> Redith the legende of martyrs of Cupide
> Which that Chaucer in Order as they stood,
> Compyled of women that wer callyd good.

Queen Anne and *The Legend of Good Women*

> *This poet wrote at the request of the queen*
> *A legend of perfect holiness*
> *Of good women, of whom he should find nineteen*
> *Who excelled in kindness and beauty;*
> *But despite all his work and effort*
> *It was too intolerable a task for his mind*
> *To find, in all the world, so great a number ...*
> *Read the legends of Cupid's martyrs*
> *Which Chaucer, one after the other,*
> *Compiled of women who were called good.*

Lydgate's assertion was widely and readily accepted as fact. Indeed, as late as 1933, Robinson wrote that:

> ... it has been not unreasonably suggested [that] Chaucer's defence of good women may have been called forth by actual condemnation of *Troilus*.
>
> *Robinson (1933)*

This view was reinforced by the fact that there were a number of indications within *The Legend of Good Women* that Lydgate's interpretation might indeed be correct. In the first place, the poem is distinctly graceful and courtly, being written in a manner and style which would make it eminently suitable for reading at court by, to, or in the presence of women. Its treatment of the whole subject of love is more idealised, more "classical," and less realistic than that seen in *Troilus and Criseyde* which had come before it or, indeed, in *The Canterbury Tales* which came immediately afterwards.

Richard II Wearing Coronation Robes
Attributed to André Beauneveu, ca. 1394–1395

Portrait in the nave of Westminster Abbey
© Dean and Chapter of Westminster

Queen Anne and *The Legend of Good Women*

More particularly, however, there are aspects of the long *Prologue* to the poem which seem, on the face of it at least, to support Lydgate's assertion. Two versions of the *Prologue* exist, being generally referred to as the F and G versions. In the F version, now thought to have been the earlier of the two, there is what has been interpreted by some as a dedication of the poem to Queen Anne:

> And wan this book ys maad, yive it the quene,
> On my byhalf, at Eltham or at Sheene.
>
> *And when this book is done, give it to the queen,*
> *On my behalf, at Eltham or at Sheen.*

Eltham and Sheen were both royal residences. Sheen, as mentioned earlier (pp. 10 & 123), was the manor house so beloved of Queen Anne, where she and Richard passed so much time together. That the queen referred to by the F *Prologue* is to be identified with Anne, appears to be confirmed by the fact that, after her death in 1394, the *Prologue* was revised by Chaucer and the new version (the G version) carried no reference to the presentation of the book to the queen "at Eltham or at Sheen."

The F *Prologue* goes even further in royal references. Chaucer commences with a very long discourse upon the daisy: after first describing the flower in fulsome detail, he then begins to refer to it in other, quite different, terms – much as a subject might speak of his queen. He talks, for instance, of being "in service" to the flower, and of the flower itself as being "the mistress of my wit." He begs the flower to be his "guide and lady sovereign," and later, when he dreams that the daisy transforms itself into a beautiful lady, later revealed to be Alceste (Alcestis: see pp. 20, 34 and 46) who is being led over the field by the god of Love, he composes a ballad to her in the formal French verse style which would have been very familiar to Queen Anne and the members of her court.

Is, then, the Alceste of the poem, who goes on to command Chaucer to write *The Legend of Good Women*, to be identified with Queen Anne who, according to Lydgate was the one who *actually* did the commanding? Perhaps. But, as it is then Alceste who tells Chaucer that he is to present the finished book to the Queen "at Eltham or at Sheen," does she not thereby distinguish between herself and Queen Anne? The question has never been answered.

Writing a poem under a degree of duress to satisfy a royal command would, one supposes, have been regarded by Chaucer – as by any author – with far less enthusiasm than undertaking a project more willingly and freely; and indeed some evidence has been adduced from *The Legend of Good Women* that Chaucer, seeing the undertaking as a chore, attempted to get through the writing as quickly as possible by using various devices to keep the whole thing as short as he could make it.

Queen Anne and *The Legend of Good Women*

Skeat was one of the first to put forward in any detail the view that Chaucer became thoroughly bored with the task of composing *The Legend of Good Women* after the *Prologue* had been completed:

> I suppose that Chaucer went on with one tale of the series after another during the summer and latter part of the same year [1385] till he grew tired of the task, and at last gave it up in the middle of a sentence.
>
> *Skeat (1889)*

The idea caught on, and other scholars began to write in the same vein. Thomas Lounsbury (1892), for example, observed that:

> There is nothing more peculiar in the "Legend of Good Women" than the steadily growing dissatisfaction of the author with his subject ….
>
> *Lounsbury (1892)*

Certainly, there is considerable evidence within *The Legend of Good Women* that Chaucer was far from being enamoured with the project. Not least of these strands of evidence is the brevity of the whole work – *The Legend of Cleopatra* comprises a mere 126 lines. It is then followed by the legends of *Thisbe* (218 lines), *Dido* (444), *Hypsipyle and Medea* (312), *Lucrece* (196), *Ariadne* (342), *Philomela* (166), *Phyllis* (168), and finally *Hypermnestra* (162) – the latter being very obviously left uncompleted (see pp. 137).

Chaucer's *The Legend of Cleopatra*

Time and again, in the course of this *Legend* or that, the narrative seems to be deliberately cut short. Thus, in what appears to be a fit of exasperation, Chaucer brushes aside Cleopatra's wedding and associated festivities:

> And, for to maken shortly is the beste,

> *And (for it is best to tell it briefly).*

His apparent irritation with the subject matter, rather than with the composition of poetry *per se*, is then immediately demonstrated by the next eight lines which explain in detail the necessity for keeping things short – a digression which advances the story not at all and also makes his excuse for omitting the details of Cleopatra's wedding to Antony – surely a crucial element in the story – seem thin and unconvincing. His further excuse that he might otherwise underplay, or even forget to mention, more important matters, seems flimsy at best.

> The wedding and the feste to devyse,
> To me, that have y-take swiche empryse
> Of so many a story for to make,
> Hit were to long, lest that I sholde slake
> Of thing that bereth more effect and charge;
> For men may overlade a ship or barge;
> And forthy to theffect than wol I skippe
> And al the remenant, I wol lete hit slippe.

> *To describe the wedding and the festivities,*
> *To me, who has undertaken the task*

Queen Anne and *The Legend of Good Women*

> *Of telling so many stories,*
> *Would take too long, in case I should understate*
> *Things of more importance and significance;*
> *For men may overload a ship or barge;*
> *And so I will therefore skip to the important matters*
> *And I will drop the rest.*

In contrast with his dismissal of the wedding, Chaucer devotes a substantial portion of his poem to a description of the Battle of Actium; this could be seen as yet another device to digress from the subject of the *Legend*, rather than as having any direct relevance to Cleopatra herself (although, as Schofield has suggested – see Chapter 8 – it may, indeed, be the most important feature of the poem).

By the time he comes to *The Legend of Philomela* (the seventh legend), Chaucer's patience, already sorely tried, would seem to be wearing even thinner:

> But, shortly of this story for to passe,
> For I am wery of him for to telle
>
> *But, to make this story pass more quickly*
> *Because I am weary of telling it …*

By legend eight, *The Legend of Phyllis*, his irritability and exasperation appear to be fairly blossoming:

> But, for I am agroted here-biforn
> To wryte of hem that been in love forsworn,
> And eek to haste me in my legende,
> Which to performe God me grace sende;
> Therefor I passe shortly in this wyse …

Chaucer's *The Legend of Cleopatra*

But I am surfeited
With writing about those perjured by love,
And I ache to tell my story quickly
Which God help me to complete!
Therefore I shall tell it briefly, like this ....

Another line of argument which has been put forward to support the view that Chaucer became tired of writing *The Legend of Good Women* is that he may originally have intended to include many more stories of "good women" in his catalogue of love's martyrs than eventually proved to be the case. At the end of *The Canterbury Tales* there is a short section, referred to as the *Retraction*, in which Chaucer writes of his regret at having written books that might, either in their subject matter or their manner of writing, have given offence to God, and which he now wishes to retract. In this *Retraction* he calls *The Legend of Good Women* "the book of the *xxv* Ladies," though the stories of only nine women appear in it. In some of the early manuscripts the number is variously given as *xv* or *xiv* (see p. 20, and also John Lydgate's comment as noted on p. 126).

The notion that Chaucer's brevity in recounting the legends, and particularly *The Legend of Cleopatra*, was the product of his distaste for the whole project, whilst plausible, is not the only explanation that has been put forward. Percival (1998), for example, has advanced the alternative view that it provided Chaucer with an excuse for omitting material which was inimical to the theme of "goodness" in the women about whom he was writing. In the *Prologue* to *The Legend of Good Women*, the god of Love, after first commanding Chaucer:

> At Cleopatre I wol that thou beginne
> *I want you to begin with Cleopatra*

adds that he should

> Sey shortly, or he shal to longe dwelle
> *Tell it succinctly, or it will take too long.*

Could this, asks Percival, be

> ... an open invitation to expurgation, spoken as it is by the God of Love in connection with Cleopatra, who has been called "the greatest courtesan in history," or, in the words of John of Salisbury and Boccaccio, the "poisonous whore (*meretrix venema*)?"
>
> *Percival (1998)*

Percival further suggests that, in Chaucer's statement

> ... forthy to theffect than wol I skippe
> And al the remenant, I wol lete hit slippe
>
> *... I will therefore skip to the important matters
> And I will drop the rest,*

the "rest" that Chaucer will let drop may refer to all those salacious details of Cleopatra's life which would disqualify her from inclusion in the group of "good" women of whom the *Legends* are to tell.

Two other matters have been seen as suggesting that writing *The Legend of Good Women* was not of Chaucer's own choosing. Firstly, he appears to have commenced work on what was to become his best-known poem, *The Canterbury Tales*, while the writing of *The Legend of Good Women* was still in its relatively early stages. Could it be that, having decided to construct the *The Legend of Good Women* as a *Prologue* followed by a series of separate stories linked only by the over-riding theme of their being concerned with "good women," he began to recognize the possibilities of the format, and that it was this recognition which stimulated him to commence work straight away on *The Canterbury Tales*? This latter employs exactly the same structure, i.e., a *Prologue* followed by a number of quite separate stories linked thematically – in this case, all of them being recounted by pilgrims on their way to Canterbury. If Chaucer's interest had been so fired by *The Canterbury Tales*, it is argued, his work on *The Legend of Good Women* might soon have become an increasingly onerous and irritating burden, to be brought to an end with as little effort as possible.

A second, and possibly more compelling, argument for Chaucer's lack of interest in *The Legend of Good Women* is that the work was left unfinished, with the final legend,

The Legend of Hypermnestra, coming to an abrupt end with the words:

> This tale is seid for this conclusioun ...
>
> *This story is told to draw the following conclusion ...*

No conclusion follows, however; nor do the usual words "*Explicit Legende* ..." ("Here ends the Legend ...").

Even this apparent incompleteness of the work does not strike everyone as conclusive. Despite the foregoing evidence suggesting that Chaucer was disenchanted by the task of writing the *Legend of Good Women* and tried, wherever possible, to keep it short, there are those, such as R. W. Frank (1972), who, after subjecting the notion to detailed scrutiny, have rejected it entirely. This view was endorsed by M. C. E. Shaner in his *Introduction* to the poem in the 2008 edition of *The Riverside Chaucer*. It is suggested by both Frank and Shaner that Chaucer could merely have been employing several perfectly appropriate rhetorical devices in order to push his stories along at a suitable pace. Moreover, at least two of his other works, including the *House of Fame* and *The Canterbury Tales*, seem also not to have been finished in accordance with their planned formats. In any case, boredom, irritation, or distaste for the subject, are only three out of a number of possible reasons for any author's decision to discontinue writing a book.

Conclusions

Did Queen Anne command – or did she, at least, strongly encourage – Chaucer to write *The Legend of Good Women*? The evidence that she may have done so is there, but it is circumstantial at best. It may be that Anne's influence was less direct: perhaps Chaucer simply desired to write a courtly poem in a style that would please the queen and meet with her approval. The question remains open.

The Deaths of Antony and Cleopatra
From a 15th century French translation of De Casibus Vivorum Illustrium, by Giovanni Boccaccio. © British Library Board; Royal 14 E V, f.339

Cleopatra putting snakes to her breast is an oft-repeated motif in mediaeval illustrations – an eroticizing theme possibly reflected in Chaucer's description of her leaping naked into a snake-filled pit.

8

Chaucer's Account of the Battle of Actium

A detailed analysis of Chaucer's description of the Battle of Actium has been presented by William Henry Schofield, who comments that:

> By far the most striking part of Chaucer's first legend [the Legend of Cleopatra], the graphic description of Antony's sea battle at Actium, is unparalleled in any "old author" from Plutarch to Boccaccio.
>
> *Schofield (1913)*

It is Schofield's primary thesis that the remarkable vividness of Chaucer's account rests upon his use of a curious amalgam of ancient events and what were, at the time of his writing, essentially anachronistic elements chosen specifically to appeal to his contemporary readership (or listeners – see the illustration on p. 7 and Note 40, p. 88) at a time when naval encounters, actual or threatened, were of crucial importance to the country. When Chaucer was starting to write *The Legend of Good Women* around 1385–1386, English sailors had already been involved in numerous maritime engagements, and it is certain that Chaucer would have heard many first-hand accounts of these from actual naval combatants. Moreover, England was at that time facing the possibility of a French naval invasion, and the common talk, particularly in London, would have been of naval warefare in all its aspects.

Schofield's analysis

Schofield makes much of the marked similarities between Chaucer's account of the Battle of Actium and descriptions of several other naval battles given in the writings of Jean Froissart. Froissart (1337–1405), a French historian who lived at the same time as Chaucer, is best known for his long and detailed prose history of the Hundred Years' War between the English House of Plantagenet and the French House of Valois, which was fought from 1337 to 1453. This work, entitled *Froissart's Chronicles*, took the form of well over one hundred manuscripts arranged into four books, and dealt in detail with all the major naval engagements up to 1400; it would undoubtedly have been available to Chaucer.

Amongst Froissart's descriptions of sea battles, most relevant to Schofield's analysis are those of the Battle of Sluys (24 June, 1340), the Battle of Les Espagnols-sur-Mer (29 August, 1350) and the Battle of La Rochelle (22 and 23 June, 1372). The phrasing used in these accounts often closely resembles Chaucer's wording in *The Legend of Cleopatra*.

Chaucer's Account of the Battle of Actium

Thus, when Chaucer writes

> Antonius was war, and wol nat faile
> To meten with thise Romains, if he may
>
> *Antony knew of this, and did not wish to avoid*
> *Engaging with these Romans, if he could,*

we may, perhaps, see an echo of the description which Froissart gives of the Battle of Les Espagnols-sur-Mer, in which the English fleet joined battle with, and defeated, a somewhat smaller fleet of Castillian (Spanish) ships: in Froissart's account it is described how the English, in response to a rallying call by Edward III, "were eager to engage the Spaniards."

Writing of the Battle of Sluys, Froissart says that, after an initial exchange of arrows, "there came shouts and cries" and "great noises from trumpets and many other types of instrument." These, and similar phrases which occur in his account of the Battle of La Rochelle, such as "shoutings and great noise" and "a great noise of trumpets and of drums," may have influenced Chaucer's line:

> Up goth the trompe – and for to shoute and shete
>
> *The trumpet sounds – and shouting and shooting.*

Chaucer makes the point that Antony oriented his fleet so that his sailors could hold the sun at their ships' sterns, and, just as importantly, keep its rays in the eyes of their enemies:

Chaucer's *The Legend of Cleopatra*

> And peynen hem to sette on with the sonne.
>
> *And they take care to keep their backs to the sun.*

Froissart, in his description of the Battle of Sluys, notes that Edward III took similar precautions when his sailors found that "the sun shone directly into their faces, which they thought would disadvantage them."

Perhaps the most obvious of Chaucer's anachronisms comes in the line:

> With grisly soun out goth the grete gonne.
>
> *With a terrible sound the great gun fires*

Although the use of cannons was a common feature of fourteenth-century sea battles, explosives were, of course, unheard of in Roman times. Whilst many attempts have been made to rationalise Chaucer's use of "gonne" to mean some form of war-engine designed to hurl rocks (see Note 20, pp. 79 & 80, for example), Schofield may be rather nearer the truth in suggesting that Chaucer was deliberately enlivening his account by using images which would be familiar and exciting to his readers or listeners.

When Chaucer goes on to say that:

> And fro the top doun cometh the grete stones.
>
> *And from above fall the great stones,*

this may be read as a description of rocks being flung by huge catapults mounted on the decks of the ships, but an alternative explanation may be indicated by Froissart's account of the Battle of Espagnols-sur-Mer, in which it is described how the Spanish ships carried large rocks and flints in containers "near the tops of their masts." These could be retrieved at an appropriate time and flung down upon the English sailors from the decks of the Spanish ships, which were much higher than those of the English vessels.

Chaucer's description of the grappling- and shearing-hooks is particularly vivid:

> In goth the grapenel so ful of crokes
> Among the ropes, and the shering-hokes.
>
> *In go the grapnels so full of claws*
> *Among the ropes, and the shear-hooks, too.*

Froissart says that in the Battle of Sluys the ships had "large grapnels and iron hooks on chains," and again, in the Battle of Les Espagnols-sur-Mer, that one ship bore down upon another and then "grappled with chains and hooks." In regard to the shearing-hooks, Froissart says that in the Battle of Les Espagnols-sur-Mer one of the sailors leapt onto an enemy ship and used his sword to "cut the large cable holding the mainsail" and followed this act by severing four more of the principal ropes. The actions of this sailor allowed the English vessels to attack the now motionless ship and, in the course of the violent fighting which then followed, the Spanish sailors were "all of them killed or thrown overboard." As Chaucer says in one particularly vivid passage in which he describes the actions of combatants in the Battle of Actium:

> In with the polax presseth he and he;
> Behynd the mast beginneth he to flee,
> And out agayn, and dryveth him over-borde ...

> *One man with a battle-axe pushes against another,*
> *Who starts to run behind the mast,*
> *And then out again, driving the other man overboard.*

Now, what are we to make of Chaucer's account of the apparently ludicrous actions of a man who appears on deck waving a goblet of wine, shouting encouragement, and telling everyone to cheer up?

> He bringeth the cuppe, and biddeth hem be blythe

> *One holds a goblet, and bids them all be cheerful*

It is interesting, and perhaps significant, to note here that Froissart, in describing the Battle of Les Espagnols-sur-Mer, reports that King Edward III "commanded wine to be brought, which he and his knights drank."

Following the goblet-waving incident, there occurs an even more curious one – the pouring of peas onto the decks, with the apparent intent of making them slippery:

> He poureth pesen upon the hacches slider

> *One pours peas on the hatches, making them slippery*

Schofield provides a critical and penetrating analysis of this line. As already observed (see Note 29, p. 83), the act of making the hatches slippery on one's own vessel – by pouring peas on them or by any other means – would diasadvantage both invading and defending sailors alike. In any case, Chaucer does not make it clear upon whose hatches the peas are being poured: if upon those of the attacking ship, then that would certainly hamper the movements of the invaders, but the usual reading is that the peas were poured by the sailor onto the deck of his *own* ship. Moreover, it is not said that the peas were poured on the hatches to *make* them slippery, but only that they *were* slippery, in which case the pouring of peas upon them must have been for some other purpose. Such a line of argument then raises the further question of whether "pesen" did actually refer to "peas" or perhaps to something else.

Here, Schofield's analysis is particularly interesting. He quotes a passage from Jean de Meun's *Le Livre de Végèce de l'Art de Chevalerie*, a 1284 translation of *De Re Militari* by Publius Flavius Vegetius Renatus (5th Century AD), which describes how an enemy vessel's deck might have pots of "pois resine et d'autres nourrisemens as feus" poured upon it. According to Schofield, "pois," as it is used here means "pitch'" which was spead upon the enemy ship in order to nourish and spread fire, thereby destroying the vessel. It could, Schofield continues, be the mistranslation of the Mediæval French "pois" as "peas" which led to the erroneous belief that it was the latter which would have been poured on the enemy ship's deck. Certainly, this line of argument is compelling, particularly as Chaucer was clearly conversant with the writings of Jean de Meun, having, as has been noted earlier (p. 5), translated the French writer's *Roman de la Rose*.

At the end of the Battle of Actium, Anthony is defeated and his forces scattered:

> Anthony is shent, and put him to the flighte,
> And al his folk to-go, that best go mighte.
>
> *Antony is beaten, and put to flight,*
> *And all his men escape as best they can.*

This finds a certain resonance in Froissart's phrasing, when he says that, after the Battle of Sluys, all those Spanish sailors who had not perished with their ships "saved themselves by flight."

Conclusions

Schofield's detailed comparison of the picture painted by Chaucer of the Battle of Actium, and the wording used in various parts of Froissart's *Chronicles* in descriptions of various naval battles, certainly suggests that Chaucer's account was couched in terms designed to appeal to his mediæval audience. As Schofield says:

Chaucer's Account of the Battle of Actium

> ... Chaucer's sea-battle is of an almost wholly mediæval sort. The methods of naval warfare that he depicts correspond in the main to those actually used by mariners in his own land when he wrote the poem .... It is likely that the poet was influenced by what he had read of sea-battles ... but he probably gained most of his information from oral accounts of recent conflicts .... [He undertook] to paint a vivid struggle between two fleets, which he knew would appeal to his readers the more it seemed to them lifelike, and answered to their preconception of what such a picture should present.
>
> *Schofield (1913)*

It is interesting in this respect to draw a comparison between the ways in which Antony and Cleopatra have been depicted in literature and art. In many paintings, Cleopatra is shown dressed in a manner wholly unlike any that she would have worn in her own time (see the illustrations on pp. 40, 73, 108, 138, 157 and 166); this may be a device to represent Cleopatra's character in a manner which would be immediately understood at the time that the painting was produced.

Some paintings of Antony also show him dressed in a manner which is appropriate to the time of the painting, rather than to the age in which he himself lived (see the illustration on p. 138); that this occurs less frequently than in paintings of Cleopatra may be because Antony is almost always depicted wearing full Roman military dress, which would have been instantly recognisable in any age. Moreover, many historical accounts of Antony specifically draw attention to his military attire – or, indeed, to the scandal which greeted his abandonment of it in favour of the Hellenistic attire of the Ptolemies during his sojourns with Cleopatra in Ephesus and Alexandria. The accounts given by historians of Cleopatra, however, concentrate on her actions and her influence upon the course of history, seldom, if ever, mentioning her mode of dress – thereby leaving the matter open to interpretation by the artists who represented her in paintings.

Aureus with the head of Antony (ca. 41 BC)

Image © Heritage Auctions, Dallas, TX

This image of Antony is typical of those found on many other coins of the period, and presents him as a heavy-set soldier and not at all effeminate – as Octavian and his propagandists were claiming before and after the Battle of Actium.

9

Sources of *The Legend of Cleopatra*

There has been considerable debate amongst scholars of Middle English literature as to the source that Chaucer used when constructing *The Legend of Cleopatra* (or, of course, sources – because there can be no certainty that he did not consult the work of more than one author). As Frank (1972) has remarked, this uncertainly has proved particularly frustrating:

> Not knowing precisely what materials he used, we cannot determine their effect on the narrative he created.
>
> *Frank (1972)*

Possible sources are noted briefly below, whilst in Appendices I, II and III passages are presented from the works of the three major contenders – Florus, Vincent de Beauvais and Boccaccio – followed by explanatory notes (see also Notes 30, 32 and 35, pp. 85–87).

The Roman historians

As Quinn (1994) notes, *The Legend of Cleopatra* is the only one of the nine poems in *The Legend of Good Women* which is not substantially derived from the works of either Virgil or Ovid.

Chaucer would certainly have been quite familiar with Plutarch's *Life of Marcus Antonius*, a highly readable biographical account appearing in his *Lives of the Noble Greeks and Romans*, written in the late first century AD. Similarly, he would have had ready access to the *Historia Romana* of Dio Cassius and the work of the same title by Appian. All these would have been in Latin, a language with which, as noted earlier, Chaucer would certainly have had some facility (pp. 3–4). However, it seems most likely that none of these was Chaucer's primary source. Several clues to this are to be found in the structure of the story, and particularly in Chaucer's inclusion of some details which are not in accord with the accounts given by the Roman historians.

Thus, in describing Cleopatra's escape after the Battle of Actium Chaucer says that her ship had purple sails (*velum purpureum*). Secondly, in the poem Antony kills himself immediately after that battle, and not – as most of the authoritative sources would have it – in Egypt around a year later. Thirdly, whilst Chaucer speaks of Cleopatra throwing herself into a pit of snakes, Plutarch mentions only a single asp. Finally, Chaucer's assertion, which is central to his poem's theme, that Cleopatra and Antony were married, is denied by the Roman historians (is this, one wonders, at least part of the reason behind Chaucer's having given the wedding ceremony such short shrift?).

Sources of *The Legend of Cleopatra*

Lucius Annæus Florus

It is possible that Chaucer took the detail of the purple sails (pp. 85–86, 62 & 84) from Lucius Annæus Florus (also – and perhaps more accurately – known as Publius Annius Florus) (75–130 AD). In his *Epitome Rerum Romanorum*, a short account of the history of Rome based loosely on Livy's writings, though omitting numerous important details, Florus wrote that:

> Cleopatra led the retreat, fleeing into the open sea in her golden ship with its purple sails.
> *Lucius Annæus Florus*

Florus could also be Chaucer's source of the historically incorrect timing of Antony's suicide (if interpreted in a particular way) and also of the dramatic version of Cleopatra's suicide involving multiple snakes. Florus did not, however, mention Antony's rejection of Octavian's sister Octavia, or marriage between Antony and Cleopatra, both of which details Chaucer did include; it is for this latter reason that doubt has been cast by some scholars upon the suggestion that Florus was the primary source of Chaucer's information about Cleopatra.

Vincent de Beauvais

Although marriage between Antony and Cleopatra may well have taken place, such a union would not have been recognised in Rome, where only a marriage between a Roman man and a Roman woman was seen as having any legitimacy; it is, however, explicitly mentioned by Vincent de Beauvais (born ca. 1200) in his *Speculum Historiale* (*The Mirror of History*), as is Antony's rejection of Octavia, both being details which Florus omitted. On the basis of such considerations, the work of Vincent de Beauvais is now widely regarded as Chaucer's most likely source (see Appendix II). Such a view is strengthened by Vincent's reference to the purple sails of Cleopatra's ship (Note 30, pp. 85–86; illustrations pp. 62 & 84).

These points, together with the brevity of Chaucer's account, which is also consistent with his having relied upon the writings of Vincent, are not, however, the only evidence for this having been his primary source. The matter would seem to be placed beyond doubt by a brief passage in the G version of the *Prologue* to *The Legend of Good Women*, in which the god of Love advises Chaucer to consult Vincent's "Storial Mirour" (*The Historical Mirror*, or *The Mirror of History* – the *Speculum Historiale*):

> What seith also the epistels of Ovyde
> Of trewe wyves, and of hir labour?
> What Vincent, in his Storial Mirour?
>
> *What do the stories of Ovid also say*
> *About faithful wives and their troubles?*
> *What does Vincent, in his Mirror of History?*

Sources of *The Legend of Cleopatra*

Although Ovid is mentioned in these lines, we have already noted (p. 149) that Quinn (1994) ruled him out as being the primary source of *The Legend of Cleopatra*, thus leaving Vincent's account as that upon which Chaucer is most likely to have based his poem. This conclusion is further strengthened by the existence of a fourteenth-century French translation of the *Speculum Historiale*, to which Chaucer could well have had access.

As Pauline Aitken (1938) has noted, however, Vincent clearly owed many of the details of his account to Florus, and it is, of course, perfectly possible that Chaucer consulted Florus's work as well as that of Vincent.

Giovanni Boccaccio

Giovanni Boccaccio (1313–1375) gave an account of Cleopatra in his *De Mulieribus Claris* (*Concerning Famous Women*), in which, like Vincent, he not only made explicit mention of a marriage between Antony and Cleopatra, but also referred to the purple sails (Note 30, pp. 85–86, and illustrations pp. 62 & 84), and it is primarily for these reasons that Boccaccio has also been proposed as one of Chaucer's sources (Appendix III). However, whilst he, like Florus and Vincent, referred to Cleopatra's attempted seduction of Octavian, Chaucer did not.

The general plan of *The Legend of Good Women* may have been influenced by Boccaccio's *De Mulieribus Claris*, with which Chaucer would certainly have been familiar, and also, in its use of a *Prologue* followed by a series of stories linked by an over-arching theme, by Boccaccio's *Decameron*. In addition, Chaucer is known to have shared Boccaccio's interest in Ovid's poetry, and probably spoke, or at least read, Italian passably well, like many educated English people at that time.

It is particularly interesting that Boccaccio, after referring to the marriage of Cleopatra and Antony, adds "I shall not go into details about ... the drunken revels." Perhaps this influenced Chaucer's lines:

> The wedding and the feste to devyse ...
> Hit were to long
>
> *To describe the wedding and the feast ...*
> *Would take too long.*

Nevertheless, there are so many differences between Chaucer's and Boccaccio's accounts that even if much of the *form* of *The Legend of Cleopatra* had been based on Boccaccio's work, the greater part of its *substance* was probably derived from elsewhere. Thus, Chaucer's description of Cleopatra's character is closer to that given by Vincent: as Frank (1972) has pointed out, if Chaucer had depended upon Boccaccio's account he would have had to ignore much that was unflattering and even insulting to Cleopatra, and which would therefore not have been suitable for the purposes of the *Legend*.

10

Is *The Legend of Cleopatra* a Poetic Success?

While *The Legend of Good Women* has given rise to much scholarly discussion and analysis, this has related mainly to *The Legend of Dido* and to the F and G versions of the *Prologue* (see p. 129), these latter being regarded as containing some of Chaucer's most interesting work. *The Legend of Cleopatra*, however, when it has been accorded any critical attention at all, has been generally dismissed as a poorly constructed poem which fails in what it purportedly attempts to do.

Why should this be? After all, there is much in *The Legend of Cleopatra* which we can admire. The passage devoted to the Battle of Actium, for example, has been rightly praised for so effectively evoking the speed and confusion of naval warfare, whilst the descriptions of Cleopatra's preparation for her death (the making of the shrine, decorated with rubies and filled with exotic spices) and of her death itself (casting herself naked into the pit of snakes), both overflow with emotional intensity.

All this is true, but in picking out this or that passage for special attention or praise could we not merely be highlighting what has been seen as the central problem

Chaucer's *The Legend of Cleopatra*

with the poem – that it lacks narrative cohesion, being little more than a package of tenuously related passages?

The title of the poem announces that it will present the story of Cleopatra, but is that what it actually succeeds in doing? Is it *truly* about Cleopatra, or is Cleopatra (or, rather, a specific period in her complex life) merely one element amongst several with which the poem deals – and not the major element at that?

Certainly, no more than 40 of the poem's 126 lines – amounting to about 32 per cent of the whole – either mention Cleopatra by name or are concerned with her actions or thoughts: Chaucer, according to Preston (1952). "skips over Cleopatra."

The first three lines do relate to Cleopatra, but only to introduce her as the heir of Ptolemy XII Auletes:

> After the deeth of Tholomee the king,
> That al Egipte hadde in his governing,
> Regned his quene Cleopataras;
>
> *After the death of Ptolemy, the king*
> *Who ruled over all Egypt,*
> *His queen, Cleopatra, reigned*

but then, with no more ado, the poem turns to Antony:

> Til on a tyme befel ther swiche a cas,
> That out of Rome was sent a senatour
>
> *Until a time came when it happened*
> *That a senator was sent from Rome.*

Is the *The Legend of Cleopatra* a Poetic Success?

Cleopatra Delivers her Life to the Serpents
From an early 15th century French translation of De Claris Mulieribus *by Giovanni Boccaccio. © British Library Board, Royal 16 G V, f.101*

A total of 37 lines – a similar proportion of the poem to that devoted to Cleopatra – are given over to Antony: first to the initial description of him and of the tension which had arisen between him and Rome, and then to his bleak despair following his defeat in the Battle of Actium and his suicide immediately afterwards.

Far more lines (54, in fact – amounting to some 43 per cent of the poem) are given over to the prelude to, and the events during, the Battle of Actium. Whilst, as we have commented earlier, this section has been praised by some as an example of Chaucer's ability to write vividly, and though it clearly has *some* relevance to Cleopatra's story, it casts little light upon her historical importance, and even less upon her character as a "good woman."

Even if one accepts Sheila Delany's analysis (Delany, 1994) that at least 17 lines (just under one-third) of the Battle of Actium sequence are no more than thinly disguised descriptions of acts of sexual congress, all presented in a manner which would have been blatantly obvious to Chaucer's readers, the introduction of such imagery at this point of the poem has no obvious direct reference to Cleopatra's *personal* sexual proclivities. (And, it must be admitted, one does occasionally get the rather uneasy feeling that Delany's interpretation may stretch credulity just a little too much.)

Quinn (1994) has gone so far as to describe the battle as an "intensely overwrought naval encounter" which is "largely irrelevant" to the narrative. Frank (1972) is even more damning, concluding that:

> The passage works to no purpose here .... At most, it might have been intended to heighten the pathos of the gentle queen, caught in a brutal masculine world of war and cruelty. The effect is never achieved, if it was intended ....
>
> *Frank (1972)*

Is the *The Legend of Cleopatra* a Poetic Success?

Percival (1998) simply dismisses it out of hand, as an "egregiously lengthy piece of padding."

We have already noted the apparently anachronistic references to "shete" and "gonne" ("shooting" and "gun," respectively) which occur in the sequence devoted to the Battle of Actium (pp. 79–81). Based upon the arguments presented by Skeat (1889), it has been proposed that, in order to maintain the Romanesque tenor of the poem, these terms could be taken as relating to the rocks hurled by giant, wooden, deck-mounted catapults which the Roman warships would have carried. A number of other writers, however, have been rather less accommodating. Schofield (1913), as we have seen in Chapter 8, has asserted bluntly that Chaucer was simply describing the form taken by naval battles in his own day:

> [the] methods of naval warfare that he depicts correspond to those actually used by mariners of his own land when he wrote his poem ....
> *Schofield (1913)*

The first two-thirds of the poem are (if one includes the Battle of Actium) essentially about Antony and his actions, though even here the narrative lacks a degree of cohesiveness. There is, for example, no direct reference to Antony when the battle is being described – even though Quinn, 1994, thinks that he is referred to indirectly as the man raising a goblet of wine (pp. 82–83).

Chaucer's *The Legend of Cleopatra*

A further criticism of the poem has related to its conflicting descriptions of Antony's character. Presented to us initially as a "worthy warrior," he is later depicted as someone whose spirit is easily broken by military defeat, leaving him weak and despairing to the point of suicide:

> "Alas!" quod he, "the day that I was born!
> My worshipe in this day thus have I lorn!"
> And for dispeyr out of his witte he sterte,
> And roof him-self anoon through-out the herte
> Er that he ferther wente out of the place.

> *"I rue," he said, "the day that I was born!*
> *This day I have lost my honour!"*
> *And despair drove him out of his mind,*
> *And he at once stabbed himself through his heart*
> *Before he went out of the place of battle.*

Although it is true that the final one-third of the poem is concerned with the thoughts and actions of Cleopatra, here, too, the narative is uneven: Cleopatra's affirmation of her love for Antony has, for example, been described by Frank (1972) as possessing no more than one "evocative romantic passage," though he concedes that this is "the most 'courtly' moment of her speech":

> ... I yow swor to been al frely youre
> I mene yow, Antonius my knight!
> That never waking, in the day or night,
> Ye nere out of myn hertes remebraunce
> For wele or wo, for carole or for daunce ....

Is the *The Legend of Cleopatra* a Poetic Success?

> *... I swore to you that I would willingly be yours –*
> *I mean you, Antony my knight! –*
> *That never, whist awake, in the day or night,*
> *Were you ever out of my heart's memory*
> *In happiness or sorrow, in song or in dance.*

This is followed by Cleopatra's extended and, it has to be said, somewhat rambling recitement of the "covenant," or pledge, which she had made to herself:

> And in my-self this covenant made I tho,
> That, right swich as ye felten, wele or wo,
> As ferforth as hit in my power lay,
> Unreprovable unto my wyfhood ay,
> The same wolde I felen, lyf or deeth,
> And thilke covenant, whyl me lasteth breeth,
> I wol fulfille, and that shall wel be sene;
>
> *And I then made this pledge to myself*
> *That whatever you were to feel, happiness or sorrow,*
> *Inasmuch as it lay in my power,*
> *Ever faithful to my wifely duty,*
> *I wished to feel the same – in life or death.*
> *And, whilst I still draw breath, that very pledge*
> *I shall fulfil, and that shall be clearly seen.*

Quinn (1994) describes this as being a

> surprisingly long and equally illogical prolegomenon to suicide [and] a complaint and a boast that also reads like the last will and testament of an incompetent contract lawyer.
>
> *Quinn (1994)*

Chaucer's *The Legend of Cleopatra*

Just as the poem's depiction of Antony's character is inconsistent, swinging between assertions of his valour and what can only be described as his lack of fibre, the same may also be said of its treatment of Cleopatra – her courageous acceptance of her own death by suicide

> ... she her deeth receyveth, with good chere.
> *... she receives her death cheerfully*

being at marked variance with her terrified flight from the Battle of Actium:

> Fleeth eek the queen, with al her purpre sail,
> For strokes, which that wente as thikke as hail;
> No wonder was, she mighte hit nat endure ....
> To Egipte is fled, for drede and for distresse;
>
> *So, too, fled the queen, with her purple sails,*
> *From the missiles which fell as thick as hail;*
> *It was no wonder she could not endure it ....*
> *[She] fled to Egypt, in fear and distress.*

Here, says Frank (1972), she seems

> ... a gentle, timorous creature, properly passive and colourless.
>
> *Frank (1972)*

A curious feature of the poem is the manner of Cleopatra's death. The story that she committed suicide by allowing herself to be bitten by an asp would certainly have been well known to Chaucer, yet he describes her flinging herself naked into a pit full of such snakes. Why,

Is the *The Legend of Cleopatra* a Poetic Success?

one wonders, did he feel it necessary to make such a dramatic adjustment to the story? Kiser (1983) has made the interesting suggestion that Chaucer may have been attempting to conjure up a vision of Cleopatra's descent into hell, thus setting her death firmly in the context of the deaths of other women "martyrs to love." The proposal is appropriate, in that the fate of Alcestis, the consort of the god of Love, and the one who, in the *Prologue*, commands Chaucer to write the legends of "good women," was to descend into the underworld. Though Cleopatra's death as described by Chaucer does not accord with the way in which it is usually depicted, it stands as one of the most memorable and dramatic moments in the poem.

When Chaucer draws near to the end of *The Legend of Cleopatra* he makes the vain protest that

> ... this is storial sooth, hit is no fable.
>
> ... *this is historical fact; it is not a fable.*

As Quinn (1994) comments, however,

> Chaucer's affirmation of the legend's facticity only highlights the ... text's incredibility ....
>
> *Quinn (1994)*

After successfully building up the poem's emotional tension with the despairing suicide of Antony, followed by the exotic – not to say theatrical – suicide of Cleopatra, Chaucer takes the curious decision to close the story with three lines which have been described by Quinn (1994) as being of "comic inappropriateness":

> Now, er I fynde a man thus trewe and stable,
> And wol for love his deeth so frely take,
> I pray god lat our hedes never ake!
>
> *Now, until I find a man as true and constant as this,*
> *And who would so willingly die for his love,*
> *I pray to God that our heads shall never ache!*

What exactly was Chaucer trying to do in this closing passage of the poem? There may be some merit in the view that he could simply have meant what he said – that the task of finding anyone as faithful as Cleopatra would make one's head ache. One cannot help feeling, however, that the force of the final line is more in accord with Quinn's description of it as comic – a little light relief for Chaucer's audience, perhaps, after the heavy emotion of the immediately preceding 35 lines.

After examining the structural integrity of *The Legend of Cleopatra*, Coghill (1949) reached the conclusion that

> [Cleopatra's] tale has been too brief for us to credit or even care for her sincerity. There is not the weight of a long wooing or of an intimately revealed character to engage us at all deeply in what she says.
> *Coghill (1949)*

– a view even more cogently expressed by Frank (1972):

Is the *The Legend of Cleopatra* a Poetic Success?

> *Cleopatra*, the shortest of the narratives, is one of the least successful ... because of its extreme brevity. The hero and heroine are whisked on and off the stage and the curtain is lowered almost before we have settled into our seats .... The poem is [also] a failure ... because it lacks imaginative unity ... [and] an ethic to bind it together ... it lacks a strong central emotion to make it coalesce.
>
> *Frank (1972)*

And then, if we add the poem's multiple historical inaccuracies to these very strong indictments of its poetic inadequacies, what do we have left?

Well, quite a lot, actually. We have the first extended treatment, rather than simply a passing mention, of Cleopatra in English literature; we have a whole mix of puzzles regarding the poem's origins and sources; we are particularly intrigued by Chaucer's reasons – ironic or purely inccocent – for having included Cleopatra amongst his selection of "good women" (and putting her first, at that); we wonder whether Chaucer used brevity simply as an effective narrative device, or whether it carried some deeper significance; and we are privileged to witness both the introduction of the new "heroic couplet" into English poetry and the effective replacement of French and Latin in English literature by the everyday spoken and written language of fourteenth-century England.

Cleopatra and Octavian
Louis Gauffier, 1787–1788
© The Scottish National Gallery

Annæus Florus, Vincent de Beauvais and Giovanni Boccaccio all described an attempt by Cleopatra to seduce Octavian: she "tried to tempt him with her eyes," says Florus (p. 174). The omission of this incident by Chaucer from *The Legend of Cleopatra* is understandable if his intention was to represent Cleopatra as a "good woman," faithful to her love for Antony (pp. 26–30). In Gauffier's painting, Octavian averts his eyes from Cleopatra, in accord with the story that the queen's efforts left Octavian unimpressed: "her charms failed to overcome his self-restraint," Florus adds (p. 174). For comments on the representation of Cleopatra's dress, which here – as in many other paintings in which she features – is not in keeping with what one might have expected of an Egyptian queen in the first-century BC, see p. 147.

11

Source Materials

Aitken, P. *Chaucer's Legend of Cleopatra, and the Speculum Historiale.* Speculum, 13: 232–236, 1938.

Amy, E. F. *The Text of Chaucer's Legend of Good Women.* Haskell House: New York NY, 1918.

Andrew, M. *The Palgrave Literary Dictionary of Chaucer.* Palgrave Macmillan: Basingstoke, 2006.

Beidler P. G. *A Student's Guide to Chaucer's Middle English.* Coffeetown Press: Seattle, 2011.

Bennett, H. S. *Chaucer and the Fifteenth Century.* The Clarendon Press: Oxford, 1947.

Benson L. D. (Ed.) *The Riverside Chaucer*, 3rd Edn. Oxford University Press: Oxford, 2008.

Boccaccio, Giovanni. *De Mulieribus Claris [On Famous Women]*, 1361. [*Concerning Famous Women: translated, with an introduction and notes, by Guido A. Guarino.* Allen and Unwin: London, 1964].

Brewer, D. *Chaucer and his World.* Eyre Methuen: London, 1978.

Burnley, D. *A Guide to Chaucer's Language.* The Macmillan Press: London, 1983.

Chesterton, G. K. *Chaucer.* Faber and Faber Ltd: London, 1948.

Chute, M. *Geoffrey Chaucer of England.* E. P. Dutton & Co.: New York, 1946.

Coghill, N. *The Poet Chaucer.* Oxford University Press: London, 1949.

Davis, S., Gray, D., Ingham, P. and Hadrill, A-W. *A Chaucer Glossary.* Oxford University Press: Oxford, 1979.

Delaney, S. *The Naked Text: Chaucer's Legend of Good Women.* University of California Press: Berkeley, 1994.

Dillon, B. *A Chaucer Dictionary: Proper Names and Allusions.* G. K. Hall & Co.: Boston, 1974.

Frank, R. W. *Chaucer and The Legend of Good Women.* Harvard University Press: Cambridge MA, 1972.

Franklin, M-A. *Boccaccio's Heroines: Power and Virtue in Renaissance Society.* Ashgate Publications: Aldershot, 2006.

Hadow G. E. *Chaucer and his Times.* Williams & Norgate: London, 1914.

Hughes-Hallett, L. *Cleopatra: Histories, Dreams and Distortions.* Harper & Row: New York, 1990.

Hussey, S. S. *Chaucer: An Introduction,* 2nd Edn. Methuen: London, 1981.

Jones, P. J. *Cleopatra: A Source Book.* University of Oklahoma Press: Norman, 1971.

Kiser L. J. *Telling Classical Tales: Chaucer and the Legend of Good Women.* Cornell University Press: Ithaca, 1983.

Lounsbury, T. R. *Studies in Chaucer.* London, 1892.

Lynch, J. L. (Ed.) *Dream Visions and Other Poems: Geoffrey Chaucer.* Norton & Co.: New York, 1972.

Source Materials

Mayhew A. L. and Skeat, W. W. *A Concise Dictionary of Middle English from A.D. 1150 to 1580.* Clarendon Press: Oxford, 1888.

McMillan, A. *The Legend of Good Women.* Rice University Press: Houston, 1987.

Percival, M. F. *Chaucer's Legendary Good Women.* Cambridge University Press: Cambridge, 1998.

Preston, R. *Chaucer.* Sheed and Ward: London, 1952.

Quinn, W. A. *Chaucer's Rehersynges: The Performability of The Legend of Good Women.* The Catholic University of America Press: Washington DC, 1994.

Robinson, F. N. (Ed.) *The Complete Works of Geoffrey Chaucer.* Oxford University Press: London, 1933.

Rudd, G. *The Complete Critical Guide to Geoffrey Chaucer.* Routledge: London, 2001.

Schofield, W. H. The sea-battle in Chaucer's 'Legend of Cleopatra.' *Anniversary Papers by Colleagues and Pupils of George Lyman Kittredge.* Ginn & Co.: Boston, 139–152, 1913.

Skeat, W. W. *Chaucer: The Works of Geoffrey Chaucer,* Vol. III. Clarendon Press: Oxford, 1884.

Skeat, W. W. *Chaucer: The Legend of Good Women.* Clarendon Press: Oxford, 1889.

Tatlock, J. S. P. *The Complete Poetical Works of Geoffrey Chaucer.* Macmillan Co.: New York, 1912.

Taylor, B. The medieval Cleopatra: the classical and medieval tradition of Chaucer's *Legend of Cleopatra. Journal of Mediaeval and Renaissance Studies,* 7: 249–269, 1977.

Thompson, W. H. *Chaucer and His Times.* A. Brown & Sons: Hull, 1936.

The Raising of Antony to the Upper Window of the Tomb
Etching in The History of Cleopatra, Queen of Egypt *by Jacob Abbott (Harper & Bros., New York, 1851): coloured. Image © Marius Press*

Detail © Marius Press

The usual version of Antony's death, differing from that related by Chaucer (see pp. 40 and 130–135), is that, on being informed that Cleopatra was dead, he stabbed himself with his sword. Death came slowly, and when he learned that Cleopatra was alive and hiding in the Mausoleum, he asked to be carried there. Antony was lifted by Cleopatra and her servants through a window into the mausoleum (see detail), where he died in Cleopatra's arms.

Appendix I
The Story of Cleopatra According to Lucius Annæus Florus

Introduction

The Roman historian Lucius Annæus Florus was born in Africa around 74 AD and lived during the principates of the four emperors Trajan, Hadrian, Antoninus Pius and Marcus Aurelius. Whilst there is uncertainty surrounding the dates of the two books which together make up his *Epitome Rerum Romanorum* (*Epitome de T. Livio Bellorum omnium annorum DCC Libri duo*), the principates of either Hadrian or Marcus Aurelius are the periods most usually suggested (i.e., somewhere between 100 and 120 AD). Based upon, and being a much shortened version of, the writings of Titus Livius (Livy), Florus's *Epitome* was a popular source of Roman history in the Middle Ages, and was still widely read well into the nineteenth century.

Florus precedes his account of Octavian's war against Cleopatra with a section which deals with the generally disastrous conclusion to Antony's attempted subjugation of the Parthians. After being defeated in battle, and then subsequently afflicted by the combined effects of disease, thirst, brackish water, the heat of the Armenian sun and the cold of the Cappadocian snow, Antony's legions were, says Florus, reduced to no more than a third of their original number. After being obliged to cut up his silver plate and distribute the pieces in payment to his soldiers, Antony then begged his sword-bearer to kill him, but the servant refused. Eventually, Antony escaped through Syria after which, as Florus puts it, "by an extraordinary twist of mind, he became more arrogant than before, almost as though by having managed to escape he had actually been victorious." At the commencement of the following section of the *Epitome Rerum Romanorum*, Florus refers to this irrationality as Antony's "madness."

The text

Because this madness which had come upon Antony could not be assuaged by his having succeeded in his ambitions, it was at last brought to an end by indulgence and dissipation. When the Parthian war ended, Antony came to hate war and lived a life of enjoyment: falling in love with Cleopatra, he allowed himself to succumb to her embraces, as though all were well with his life.

As the just reward for her favours, this Egyptian woman demanded of the inebriated general nothing less than the whole of the Empire of Rome. This was promised to her by Antony, as though the Romans would be easier than the Parthians to defeat!

He thus commenced directing his aim towards the acquisition of sovereignty, and did so, indeed, in no covert manner. Disregarding his own country, his name, his Roman toga, and the fasces (the insignia of his office), he degenerated in his thoughts and in his sentiments, as well as in the manner of his dress, into a monster.

He carried in his hand a sceptre of gold, and bore a scimitar at his hip; the robe he wore was purple, decorated with great gems; only a crown was lacking that might make him appear to be a king in dalliance with a queen.

As soon as Octavian[1] had become aware of the latest reports of all these things, he had made the crossing from Brundisium to face the war that was to come; and after setting up camp in Epirus he had encircled the coast off Actium with a formidable fleet, threatening the island of Leucas and Mount Leucate, as well as the two promontories at the mouth of the Gulf of Ambracia.

Octavian[2] possessed in excess of four hundred warships; and although Antony[3] had fewer than two hundred, their size was some compensation for this because, having between six and nine banks of oars, and standing high out of the water, with towers and tall decks which made them look like castles and cities, their movement caused the sea to groan and the wind to fall fatigued. Their very size, however, was their undoing.

Octavian's[1] ships, possessing no more than two to six banks of oars, were more able to undertake any manoeuvre that might be required of them, whether this might be to attack, withdraw or wheel around. They were therefore able to engage with the heavier vessels, which were in all respects clumsier and more unwieldy, often attacking several at a time with their beaks[4] and hurling firebrands into them, thus scattering those vessels at their pleasure.

At no time was the sheer size of Antony's[3] warships more apparent than after Octavian's victory, for, after the battle had ended, wreckage of his ships was spread over the surface of the sea, together with the spoils of the victories they had won over the Arabeans, Sabæans and a thousand other Asiatic nations. The waves, fanned by the wind, continually cast up purple and gold upon the shore. Cleopatra[5] led the retreat, fleeing into the open sea in her golden ship with its purple sails[6].

Antony soon followed, but Octavian[1] was quickly upon his heels. And thus it was that neither the preparations that Antony and Cleopatra[7] had made for flight into the open ocean, nor their securing of Paraetonium and Pelusium, the two horns of Egypt, with the use of garrisoned troops, helped them at all: they were almost within Octavian's[1] grasp.

Antony was first to commmit suicide by the use of his own sword. Cleopatra[5], however, threw herself down before Octavian's[1] feet and tried to tempt him with her eyes, but the attempt was in vain, for her charms failed to overcome his[8] self-restraint.

Her efforts were directed not at preserving her life, which had been offered to her, but at acquiring a portion of the Roman empire. Despairing of receiving this from Octavian[1], and realizing that she was being spared merely to be led as a captive in his Triumph, she slipped past the negligent guard and entered the Mausoleum – which is the name given to the royal supulchre. Once there, and having donned the fine apparel, in which she was customarily dressed, she lay beside her beloved[9] Antony in a coffin which had been filled with rich perfumes, and then, by putting poisonous snakes to her veins, she died as though falling asleep.

Notes

1. "Caesar" or "Caesar's" has been rendered here as "Octavian," or "Octavian's."

2. Because the reference is clearly to Octavian's fleet, "we" is here rendered as "Octavian."

3. The original says "the enemy" or "the enemy's" which are references to Antony and his fleet.

4. "Beaks" were long, pointed battering rams mounted at the front of the ships, and with which the enemy ships were struck and their hulls pierced.

5. The original is "The queen." Cleopatra's attempted seduction of Octavian was omitted from Chaucer's poem (see pp. 25, 153, 166, 178 and 188).

6. The "golden ship with its purple sails" describes the royal barge in which Cleopatra sailed up the river Cydnus to her meeting with Antony in Tarsus, rather than any ship which she would have used in her attempt to escape from the Battle of Actium and afterwards to make the long crossing over the Mediterranean to Egypt. A similar error is made in

the accounts of both Vincent de Beauvais and Boccaccio, as well as in *The Legend of Cleopatra*. (see pp. 62 and 85–86, Chapter 9, and Appendices II and III).

7. Though the original does not specify the names of Antony and Cleopatra, the sense is clear.

8. The original is "the prince's."

9. This is the nearest Florus comes to suggesting that Cleopatra and Antony may have married. Marriage is mentioned by Vincent de Beauvais (Appendix II), Boccaccio (Appendix III) and Chaucer.

The Egyptian Cobra.
From an old print. Image © Marius Press

Asp (short for *Aspis*) is the name given to any venomous snake of the Nile, of which the cobra (*Naja haje*) is particularly common.

Appendix II

The Story of Cleopatra According to Vincent de Beauvais

Introduction

Vincent de Beauvais was born around 1180–1190 AD. A French Dominican friar, he was perhaps the greatest – and certainly the most influential – encyclopædist of the Middle Ages. Between 1220 and 1244, writing under the names of Vincentius Bellovacensis or Vincent of Burgundy he attempted to put together a systematic account of all human knowledge in a monumental work which he called the *Speculum Maius*, or *The Great Mirror*.

This consisted of three parts: the *Speculum Naturale* (*The Mirror of Nature*); the *Speculum Doctrinale* (*The Mirror of Doctrine*); and the *Speculum Historiale* (*The Mirror of History*). A fourth volume, titled the *Speculum Morale* (*The Mirror of Morals*) was added much later (probably in the fourteenth century) by an unknown author.

Although the brief account which Vincent gives of Cleopatra's involvement with Antony seems clearly to have been based upon that of Lucius Annæus Florus, it is quite substantially shorter than the Roman historian's account.

Chaucer's *The Legend of Cleopatra*

The text

Since he was lustful[1], Antony was seized with love for Cleopatra, the Queen of Egypt. Having rejected Octavian's[2] sister, joining Cleopatra to himself in marriage[3], he declared war[4] on Octavian[2]. As soon as Octavian heard the news[5] he took three hundred ships from Brundisium to Epirus. Antony had in fact occupied the Greek coast, but when it came to battle, and Octavian's[2] fleet began to spread confusion amongst Antony's ships, Queen Cleopatra, in her gilded ship with purple sails[6], was the first to flee, and Antony immediately followed her. Seeing that Octavian was close upon his heels, Antony killed himself with his own hand. Then the Queen threw herself before Octavian's[2] feet and tried to seduce him with her eyes[7], but upon being spurned by him, she despaired[8]. When she realized that she was being spared merely to be in his Triumph, and after having evaded a guard[9], going into the Mausoleum which was filled with perfumes, she lay beside her Antony. Then, after applying poisonous snakes to herself, she passed through sleep into death.

Notes

1. The only reference which Vincent makes to lustfulness in his account is in reference to Antony rather than to Cleopatra.
2. The original says "Augustus's," though this is quite clearly anachronistic. Octavian assumed the title of Augustus only some time after he had defeated Antony and Cleopatra at the Battle of Alexandria.

3. Unlike Florus (Appendix I), Vincent clearly states that Antony and Cleopatra were married; an assertion repeated in Boccaccio's account (Appendix III). See also pp.24, 26 and 150–154.

4. It was Octavian (or, more accurately, the Roman senate), and not Antony, who had declared war on Cleopatra and, therefore, only by association on Antony. Perhaps the sense here is similar to that in Chaucer's line: "For whiche he took with Rome and Cesar stryf," meaning that Antony quarrelled with both Octavian and the Roman people.

5. Although the original reads "on the first signs of fresh action" (*apud prima novorum motuum signa*) it is unclear to what this refers, as Antony made no move against Octavian at this time.

6 This inaccurate description of the ship as having been equipped with purple sails, is given by both Florus and Boccaccio (Appendices I and III), and repeated by Chaucer (see the illustrations on pp. 62 and 84; see also pp. 85 and 86)

7. Or "she tempted his eyes" (*tentavit oculos eius*).

8. Or "she gave up hope" (*desperavit*).

9. The original says "having obtained a careless guard" (*incautionem nacta custodiam*).

The *Speculum Historiale* of Vincent de Beauvais
Title page of the 1624 printed edition. Image © Marius Press.

Appendix III

The Story of Cleopatra According to Giovanni Boccaccio

Introduction

Giovanni Boccaccio, who was born in 1313 in Certaldo, Italy, began work on his *De Mulieribus Claris* (*Concerning Famous Women*) in December 1361, completing it some thirteen years later in 1374, and subsequently issuing a revised version in 1375. His book contains biographies of 106 famous women, both mythical and historical, and is generally regarded as one of his most significant works. It was written in Latin, and although it did not appear in Italian until the latter part of the fourteenth, or in a French translation until some time in the fifteenth, century, it is certain that Chaucer would have had access to the original Latin version.

Boccaccio's treatment of Cleopatra is, as has been mentioned in Chapter 2 (p. 25), exceptionally hostile, and this has been the primary justification for the generally-held view that his biography of the Egyptian queen was not Chaucer's main source of material for *The Legend of Cleopatra*. It is undeniable, however, that there are some similarities between Boccaccio's and Chaucer's accounts.

Chaucer's *The Legend of Cleopatra*

The text

Cleopatra was a woman from Egypt towards whom the gossip of the whole world was directed. Though descended, through a line of kings, from Ptolemy the son of Lagus and king of Macedonia, and though she was the daughter of King Ptolemy Dionysus (or, as some are disposed to believe, of King Minos), she rose to the height of her power by crime. Any glory that she may have gained was through little else but her beauty, and she became universally known for her avarice, cruelty and lustfulness.

To commence her story at the beginning of her reign, it is said by some that when Dionysus (an important ally of the Romans at the time that Julius Caesar held his first consulship) was close to death, he issued a testament in which he decreed that his eldest daughter, Cleopatra, was to be wed to his eldest son, Lysanias[1], and that, at his death, the two were to be co-rulers. And so it was done, for such a disgraceful thing was quite common among the people of Egypt, to whom only marriage to one's daughter or mother was prohibited. Then Cleopatra, who was consumed by the desire to rule, poisoned the innocent boy, who was a mere fifteen years of age and was both her brother and husband; and thus she ruled alone. Then Pompey the Great, after occupying the greater part of Asia Minor, came to Egypt where he substituted for Cleopatra's brother a boy[2] who had survived, and thereby made the boy the king of Egypt. Furious, Cleopatra then took up arms against him. When Pompey, after suffering defeat in Thessaly at the hands of Julius Caesar, came to Egypt he was murdered by this boy whom he had made king.

Giovanni Boccaccio

Caesar, upon arriving in Egypt, discovered the Egyptians engaged in civil war, and he commanded them to present themselves before him to plead their cases. I shall say nothing further of young Ptolemy. Cleopatra then arrived in royal splendour, exuding self-confidence and craftiness, and believing that she could regain control of her realm by drawing Caesar, the conqueror of the world, into desiring her, and being herself very beautiful and able to captivate anyone with her lustrous eyes and her eloquence, she ensnared the lustful prince into her embrace. She lay with him through many nights, whilst the tumult of Alexandria surrounded them, and, as it is generally agreed, she conceived a son to whom she gave the name Caesarion, after that of his father.

Eventually, the young Ptolemy, whom Caesar had abandoned, responded to the urging of his soldiers and, turning against the one who had liberated him, took his army to the Delta to face Mithridates of Pergamum who was marching to the aid of Caesar. It was there that Caesar, who had come by another route, defeated him, and when Ptolemy attempted to escape in a boat the vessel sank under the weight of the many men who were aboard. It was thus, after all had become quiet again and the Alexandrian people had surendered, that Caesar made preparations to move agains Pharmaces, who was the king of Pontus and had acted in support of Pompey. He then gave the kingdom of Egypt to Cleopatra, almost as though it were a payment which he owed her because of her crime: Cleopatra desired nothing else, though Caesar had first to eliminate[3] Arsinoë, her sister, in case she should cause new uprisings against him.

Chaucer's *The Legend of Cleopatra*

Thus it was that Cleopatra, now in control of her kingdom as the result of two crimes, abandoned herself to pleasure. Having by now become almost the whore of the Eastern kings, and having an insatiable appetite for gold and jewels, not only did she use her artifice to strip her lovers of all these things, but, as it was said, she also plundered the temples and all the sacred places of Egypt, taking their many vases, statues and all else of any worth. Later, after Caesar had been murdered and Brutus and Cassius had been defeated, Antony was on his way towards Syria when she went to meet him, easily luring the lustful man into her snare with her beauty and her wanton eyes. She not only ensured that he remained hopelessly in love with her, but induced him to eliminate all threats to her rule – she, who had given poison to her own brother! – by making him murder[3] her sister Arsinoë in the temple of Diana the Ephesian, where the poor girl had, for her own safety, hidden herself. And this was the first reward for her adultery that Cleopatra took from her new lover.

The wicked woman so well understood Antony's character, that she did not hesitate to demand of him the kingdoms of Syria and Arabia. It seemed to him that this would be a terrible and unseemly thing to do, but he nevertheless gave her small parts of both of those countries. And to these he added all the cities close to the Syrian coast between Egypt and the river Eleutheras, retaining Sidon and Tyre as his own. Once she had succeeded in obtaining these territories, Cleopatra then followed Antony to the Euphrates where he was conducting his campaign against the Armenians (some say the Parthians).

Giovanni Boccaccio

On her way back to Egypt she passed through Syria, and was royally received by Herod Antipater, the king of Judea. She showed no shame in sending envoys ahead of her to invite him into her embraces, and, had he accepted, she would have taken as her payment the kingdom that only shortly before had been given to him by Antony. Herod realized all this and refused her invitation, not only out of his respect for Antony but also because, having planned to slay her with his sword in order to be free of the shame of such a lewed creature, his advisors had dissuaded him from doing so. After she had failed in her real purpose, Cleopatra presented Herod with the revenue of Jericho, as though this had been her only reason for calling on him. Jericho was rich in balsalms, a plant that she later brought to Babylon in Egypt (and there it may still be found). After Cleopatra had then been presented with great gifts by Herod she left that country and returned to Egypt.

She later went to meet Antony on his return, as he was fleeing from the Parthians. Treacherously, he had seized Artavastes, the son of Tigranes and king of Armenia, as well as the king's sons and satraps[4]. From all these he had stolen great treasures, and Artavastes was brought shackled in chains of silver. As the covetous Cleopatra drew near, the effeminate[5] Antony presented to her the captive king, dressed in all his fine regalia, and gave her also the booty – and all this to draw her once again into his arms!

The grasping woman, who was delighted with the gifts, embraced the passionate man so seductively that he took her as his wife[6], and did so with great love, after having repudiated Octavia[7], who was the sister of Octavian. I shall not go into details[8] about the Saban perfumes, and the drunken revels.

As Antony continually gorged gluttonously with great delicacies, he asked to know what magnificent item might be added to the daily banquets, wanting – or so it seemed – to make the meals more splendid for Cleopatra. The lewd woman responded that, if he so desired, she would command that a dinner be prepared that would cost over one hundred thousand sesterces. Antony believed that this was not possible, but, wishing both to see and taste such a feast, he replied that she should try to do so. On the following day, when the feast was not out of the ordinary, and Antony had begun to cast scorn upon her, Cleopatra asked her servants to produce the next course. In accordance with the instructions that they had been given, they brought a single goblet containing strong vinegar. At once, Cleopatra removed a precious pearl from one of her ears where she wore it (as was the custom for Eastern women) as an ornament; then, dissolving the pearl in the vinegar, she drank from the goblet. As she began to remove a pearl of equal value from her other ear, in order to repeat what she had just done, Lucius Plautus declared Antony the loser; Cleopatra, now being the winner, preserved the second pearl, which was later brought to Rome and there placed on the ear of the statue of Venus in the Pantheon, and this was so that any who looked upon it might remember Cleopatra's supper.

As the insatiable woman's cravings for kingdoms had been growing day by day, she now asked Antony to cede to her the whole of the Roman empire, so that she might seize everything at once. He may have been drunk, or perhaps it was because he had only just risen from a splendid supper, that Antony was not in complete possession of his faculties, and, without giving any consideration to the strength of his own position, or to the might of Rome, promised to give her what she asked – as though it were truly his to give!

Good heavens! How great was the audacity of this woman who made such a request! And no less was the madness of the man who promised to fulfil that request! And how generous this man who had so rashly succumbed, and had then surrendered to this begging woman the empire which had been acquired over many centuries, and with such hardships and bloodshed, through the sacrifice of many great men – and even of peoples – and as the result of so many noble deeds and wars, as though he wished to give it away at once, as he would the ownership of a house! Need I say more? The rejection of Octavia[7] by Antony had already sown the seeds of war between him and Octavian. It was for this reason that war ensued as soon as both had mustered their forces.

Antony and Cleopatra sailed to Epirus in their fleet of ships which were all decorated with gold and bore sails of purple[9]. It was there that they entered into battle on land with the enemy, until, after being defeated, they withdrew. Embarking once more onto their ships, Antony's soldiers returned to Actium, for it was there that they would try their fortune in battle upon the sea. Then Octavian, with his son-in-law Agrippa, advanced upon them with a great fleet and with extraordinary daring. As soon as it seemed that Antony's forces faced certain destruction, proud

Cleopatra fled first – on her golden ship, accompanied by sixty other vessels. Antony lowered his praetorian ship's flag and immediately followed Cleopatra.

After they had returned to Egypt and had sent away their children to the Red Sea, they readied their forces to defend their kingdom, though it was all in vain. Octavian had pursued them and had destroyed their forces in a number of battles from which he had emerged victorious. They sued for peace at the last minute. When he was unable to secure the terms he desired, Antony fell into despair and – or so it is said by some – went into the royal mausoleum and killed himself with his own sword.[10]

When Alexandria had been captured, Cleopatra once again attempted to use her wiles to induce the young Octavian to lust for her, as she had done with Caesar and Antony. When she realized that she was to be kept alive only so that she might feature in the conqueror's Triumph, she became enraged. Donning the royal garments, she followed her Antony into the mausoleum. There, lying next to him, she opened up the veins in her arms and placed there two[11] asps, so that she might die. There are those who say that these creatures bring about death through sleep. In so sleeping, this dreadful woman brought to an end her greed, her lustfulness, and also her life.

Notes

1. Ptolemy XIII Theos Philopater, Cleopatra's brother and first husband.
2. Ptolemy XIV Theos Philopater II, Cleopatra's brother and second husband.

3. Julius Caesar "eliminated" Arsinoë by banishing her to the Temple of Diana in Ephesus, where he ordered that she should spend the rest of her days. Boccaccio is incorrect in stating that she had fled there to save her own life. When Cleopatra urged Antony to arrange Arsinoë's death, he did not, as Boccaccio implies, personally carry out the murder but ordered that she be taken from the temple in Ephesus and killed on the temple steps.

4. "Satraps" were provincial governors or subordinate rulers of territories within a kingdom.

5. This reference to Antony as being "effeminate" can only be read as reinforcing Boccaccio's portrayal of the extent of Cleopatra's malign dominance over the Roman and thus his figurative emasculation.

6. Boccaccio, like Vincent de Beauvais (Appendix II), though unlike Florus (Appendix I), is quite explicit regarding the marriage of Antony and Cleopatra, and this was repeated by Chaucer.

7. The perfunctory rejection of Octavia, the sister of Octavian, is not mentioned by Florus (Appendix I), though it is by Vincent (Appendix II) and Chaucer.

8. This technique of *abbreviatio* (quickly moving on to the next stage of a story by omitting details) at this

point in the story was also employed by Chaucer (see p. 154): Boccaccio uses the same device later when, after describing how Cleopatra had successfully begged Antony to cede more territories to her, he adds "Need I say more?"

9. This attribution of purple sails and golden hulls to Cleopatra's ship is also made by Florus and Vincent (Appendices I & II), though Boccaccio ascribes these features to all the ships in Cleopatra and Antony's fleet. Chaucer, whilst mentioning the purple sails, does not refer to the golden hull.

10. Boccaccio's version of Antony's suicide is the widely accepted one in which Antony did not, as Chaucer would have it, kill himself immediately after the Battle of Actium, but did so a year later in Egypt. It has been claimed that Chaucer's version was derived from the accounts given by Florus and Vincent (Appendices I & II), but this interpretation of their writings is certainly open to question (Note 32, p. 86), and if they were Chaucer's sources it was probably through his misreading of them.

11. Boccaccio mentions two asps, whilst both Florus and Vincent refer to unspecified numbers of snakes (see Appendices I and II). Chaucer alone speaks of a pit being filled with many snakes.

Giovanni Boccaccio

Giovanni Boccaccio
Unknown Artist, ca. 1980

From Boccaccio: The Decameron, *Easton Press (1980).*
© MBI Inc. Reproduced by permission of Easton Press, Norwalk, CT, USA.

The Chaucer family coat of arms
© *Marius Press.*